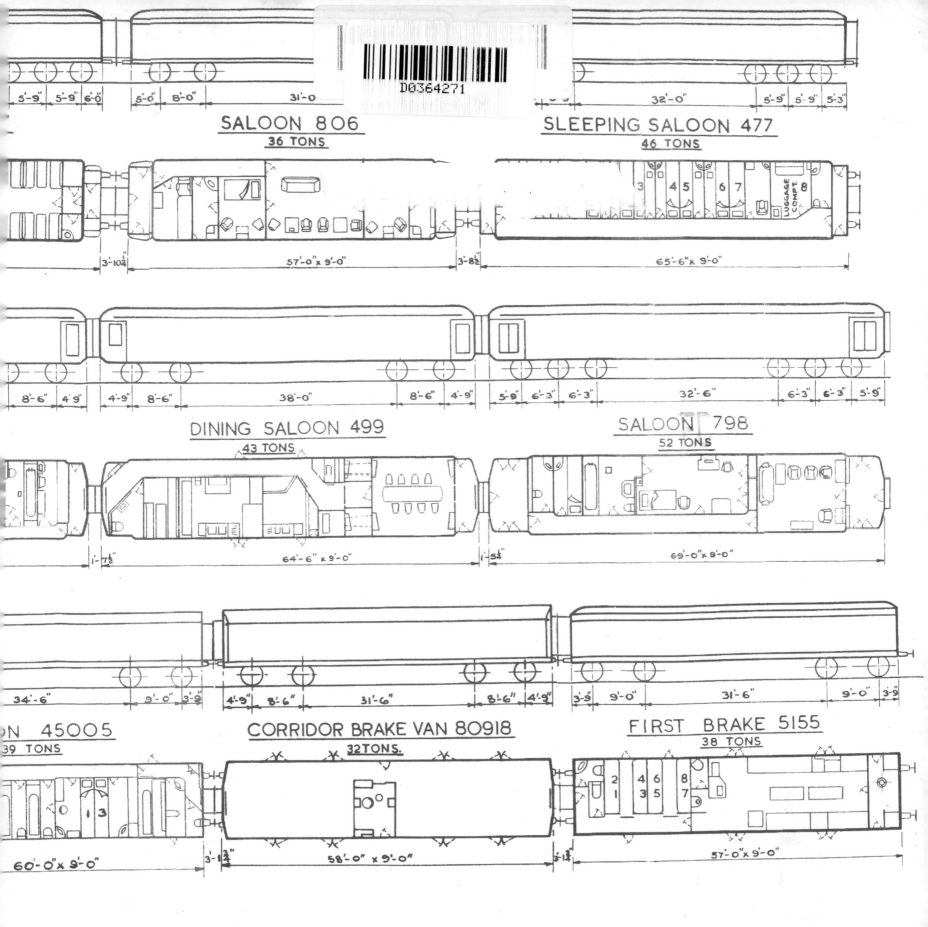

5'-9" 5'-9" 6'-0"   5'-0" 8'-0"   31'-0"   32'-0"   5'-9" 5'-9" 5'-3"

SALOON 806
36 TONS

SLEEPING SALOON 477
46 TONS

3 4 5 6 7 LUGGAGE COMPT. 8

3'-10¼"   57'-0" x 9'-0"   3'-8½"   65'-6" x 9'-0"

8'-6" 4'-9" 4'-9" 8'-6"   38'-0"   8'-6" 4'-9" 5'-9" 6'-3" 6'-3"   32'-6"   6'-3" 6'-3" 5'-9"

DINING SALOON 499
43 TONS

SALOON 798
52 TONS

1'-7½"   64'-6" x 9'-0"   1'-5¼"   69'-0" x 9'-0"

34'-6"   9'-0" 3'-9" 4'-9" 8'-6"   31'-6"   8'-6" 4'-9" 3'-9" 9'-0"   31'-6"   9'-0" 3'-9"

...ON 45005
39 TONS

CORRIDOR BRAKE VAN 80918
32 TONS.

FIRST BRAKE 5155
38 TONS

1 3

2 4 6 8
1 3 5 7

60'-0" x 9'-0"   3'-1¼"   58'-0" x 9'-0"   3'-1¼"   57'-0" x 9'-0"

The Royal Train

Other books by this author include

Zara Phillips: A Revealing Portrait of a Royal World Champion

Princess Anne

Monarchy

Invitation to the Palace

Anne: The Princess Royal

The New Royal Court

All the Queen's Men

The Queen and Her Family

Maclean of Duart

Mountbatten: The Private Story

Anne: The Private Princess Revealed

Buckingham Palace: A Guide

Diana: Princess of Wales

Charles & Diana: Portrait of a Marriage

The Royal Yacht Britannia

Her Majesty: Fifty Regal Years

Queen Elizabeth II: Jubilee edition

At Home with The Queen

Life with The Queen

William

Snowdon: Public Figure, Private Man

The Royal Train

THE INSIDE STORY

BRIAN HOEY

First published in October 2008

A catalogue record for this book is available from the
British Library

ISBN 978 1 84425 556 6

Library of Congress control no 2008926357

Published by Haynes Publishing, Sparkford, Yeovil,
Somerset BA22 7JJ, UK
Tel: 01963 442030 Fax: 01963 440001
Int. tel: +44 1963 442030 Int. fax: +44 1963 440001
E-mail: sales@haynes.co.uk
Website: www.haynes.co.uk

Haynes North America Inc., 861 Lawrence Drive,
Newbury Park, California 91320, USA

Designed by Alan Gooch
Printed and bound in Britain by J. H. Haynes & Co. Ltd.

RIGHT: *Conveying The Queen and Prince Philip to
Exeter on 1 May 2002, the Royal Train, headed by
No. 47798* **Prince Harry***, is seen passing Cockwood
Harbour, near Dawlish, Devon. (Russell Ayre)*

Contents

Author's note 9
Acknowledgements

Introduction 10

1. The Train now standing at Platform ... 20

2. Royal meals on railway wheels 36

3. The Train today 54

4. Royal progress 72

5. The cost and value 94

6. Early days 104

7. Royal funeral trains 118

8. Wolverton – home to the Royal Train 136

9. The Future 148

Appendix – Royal Train schedules 1838–2002 156

Select Bibliography 174

Index 175

Foreword

by Sir William McAlpine

*H*AVING been fascinated by all forms of rail travel since early childhood, it will come as no surprise to those who know me, to hear that I am a devoted supporter of the Royal Train and in particular, the dedicated team who operate, maintain and service the locomotives and coaches.

Railways are an addiction that is impossible to cure, and no one I know who has the habit, ever wants to recover from it. Railways become a way of life to thousands of enthusiasts and when I was bitten by the bug, a lifetime love of trains was engendered that has not diminished one iota in seven decades.

I have been fortunate enough to be able to acquire a number of historic railway coaches and engines, including two former Royal Train coaches, one of which was a sleeping car with four beds and two full bathrooms on board.

In 1842, Queen Victoria was the first British Queen Regnant to make a journey by rail – from Slough to London Paddington Station. Her Majesty went on to use her train to travel to all parts of her Kingdom during her long reign and many of the improvements made to her trains were years ahead of their introduction to normal passenger services. Queen Victoria's great-great-granddaughter, Elizabeth II, is only the second Queen Regnant to travel by Royal Train and Her Majesty uses it as a convenient and economical way to move around the United Kingdom on her official business, as does HRH The Prince of Wales, the most frequent passenger on the current Royal Train.

Wherever the Royal Train goes it still attracts an enormous amount of attention with its coaches painted in distinctive 'Royal Claret' – and on those occasions when it is pulled by a steam locomotive, it is without doubt one of the most impressive and emotive sights.

One thing is certain, the Royal Train has a wonderful future, even if the regal opulence of earlier centuries has gone forever. The present Train may not be a Palace on Wheels, but it is still by far the most comfortable, speedy and safe way for the Monarch and her family to move around the country.

Sir William McAlpine, born at The Dorchester Hotel, London, in 1936, had developed his lifelong interest in railways by the age of two. While spending all his working life in the family construction business, his hobby resulted in him rescuing The Flying Scotsman, *running charter trains and restoring engines and rolling stock at Steamtown, putting together a consortium to buy the Romney, Hythe and Dymchurch Railway, and becoming involved in too many other railways to mention here. Along the way he has rescued a vast number of railway-related buildings and artefacts, including two carriages from the Royal Train. As Chairman of the Railway Heritage Trust he is able to continue this conservation on an even wider scale. He has served on both the Southern and Western Boards of BR, is President of the Transport Trust and Chairman of the Romney, Hythe and Dymchurch Railway and the Dart Valley Railway.*

RIGHT: *When the Royal Train is pulled by a steam locomotive, as here on 11 June 2002 as part of The Queen's Golden Jubilee tour of Wales, it is one of the most impressive and emotive sights. (Chris Milner)*

ABOVE: *One of the joys of train travel is the spectacular view from the coaches. Here, the Royal Train is crossing the famous Ribblehead Viaduct on the Settle & Carlisle line on 22 March 2005. (Geoff Griffiths)*

Author's note

THIS is not a chronological account of rail travel since the early days of the 19th century. Others, far more qualified, have written many scholarly works full of technical detail that would appeal to the rail enthusiasts who are experts themselves in this field. But I have, of necessity, included chapters dealing with the history of the Royal Train, and included details of some significant journeys made by the Royal Family, and the timetables and descriptions of the current Royal saloons.

This is a book that attempts to tell the inside story of what happens when The Queen and her family travel on the Royal Train, and on 'ordinary' passenger trains, through the words of those who actually work with them. I have tried to explain the travelling habits of the Royal Family, their individual tastes and demands, and how the men who organise these journeys go to extraordinary lengths to ensure their comfort and safety. As one long-serving member of the train staff explained: 'We treat every journey as if it were the first.'

The Royal Train is as much a Royal residence as Buckingham Palace, Windsor Castle or Balmoral for Her Majesty, or Clarence House or Highgrove for the Prince of Wales: when they are on board it becomes a mobile palace, with perhaps a little less formality. Now that there is no longer a Royal Yacht, the Royal Train is arguably the most glamorous and romantic of all Royal residences and, as much of the information to which I have been allowed access is exclusive, I hope this will be seen as a unique insight into the Royal Family's life on the move.

Acknowledgements

Among the many people who have contributed to this book and helped me considerably in preparing it are members of the Royal Household and those who operate and maintain the Royal Train. At Buckingham Palace, Samantha Cohen, Press Secretary to The Queen, Ailsa Anderson, Deputy Press Secretary, and David Pogson, Information Officer, have been unfailingly courteous and cooperative, while Group Captain Tim Hewlett, Director of Royal Travel, and his colleagues were equally helpful.

My first visit to the Royal Train at Wolverton was arranged and conducted by Chris Hillyard, the Royal Train Special Vehicles Manager, who personally guided me through every aspect of Royal rail travel and gave me a splendid tour of all the Royal coaches with a unique insight that has come only with over thirty years' experience.

Geoff Griffiths, the Royal Train Account Manager at English, Welsh & Scottish Railway, and a great train enthusiast, spent many hours explaining the planning that goes into each Royal Train journey, and also provided many of the photographs in the book. Paul Higgins, at First Great Western, told me what happens when members of the Royal Family travel on 'ordinary' passenger services. My thanks also to Nigel Venneear of British Transport Police and his colleagues. However, at the request of Buckingham Palace I have not included specific details of the security measures surrounding the Royal Train.

Nick Edwards, the Royal Train Officer, who accompanies The Queen and her family on every journey, was extremely generous in sharing his time and knowledge and he arranged for me to join one of his drivers, Phil George, in the cab to talk about the skills required when handling the most famous locomotives in the world.

Roger Williams, of Rail Gourmet, gave up one of his rare free weekends to welcome me into his home and share his expertise on Royal Train catering. He also introduced me to his Chief Steward, Ken Moule, the man who knows more stories about the Royal Train than anyone else.

I would particularly like to thank Patrick Kingston for his generous and unselfish contribution. And I am very grateful to Sir William McAlpine for his gracious and generous Foreword to the book. Others to whom I owe a debt of gratitude include: Sir Richard Branson, Brian Goode, Jessica Skinner, Theresa Williams, my agent, Gordon Wise, at Curtis Brown, and especially Mark Hughes, Editorial Director at Haynes Publishing, who commissioned the book in the first place. His colleagues at Haynes – including Jeremy Yates-Round, Flora Myer, Alan Gooch, Christine Smith, Peter Nicholson and Rebecca Nicholls – have been enthusiastic supporters and used their expertise in the editing, marketing and production of the book, for which I am most thankful. If I have left anybody out I apologise, and of course, any errors are mine and mine alone.

Introduction

The Queen loves it, claiming this is one of the few places left on earth where she can literally kick off her shoes, put up her feet and relax in total privacy. Prince Philip, who likes to make the most of every minute of the day, uses it as a mobile office, while both the Prince of Wales (who says he couldn't live without it) and his sister Anne, the Princess Royal (who is no longer permitted to use it exclusively, her last 'solo' journey was on 2/3 June 1999 when she travelled overnight from London Euston to Glasgow Central) say it is their favourite form of travel now that the Royal Yacht *Britannia* is no longer in service. It is, of course, The Queen's mobile home-from-home, the Royal Train, although that description is, in itself, something of a misnomer.

The Court Circular, the official document issued daily by Buckingham Palace listing the engagements and movements of all those members of the Royal Family who undertake public duties, often reveals that one of them has travelled by 'The Royal Train', as if there is only one such vehicle. However, the phrase is applied whenever a set of rail carriages and locomotives is used

BELOW: *The lady walking along the sea wall at Dawlish in Devon during the spring of 2008 seems completely unaware that she is so close to the Royal Train, which is carrying The Queen to Totnes for a visit to the Royal Naval College at Dartmouth. The train is hauled by EWS Class 67 No. 67005* **Queen's Messenger***, one of two such modern locomotives in Royal Claret livery. (Geoff Griffiths)*

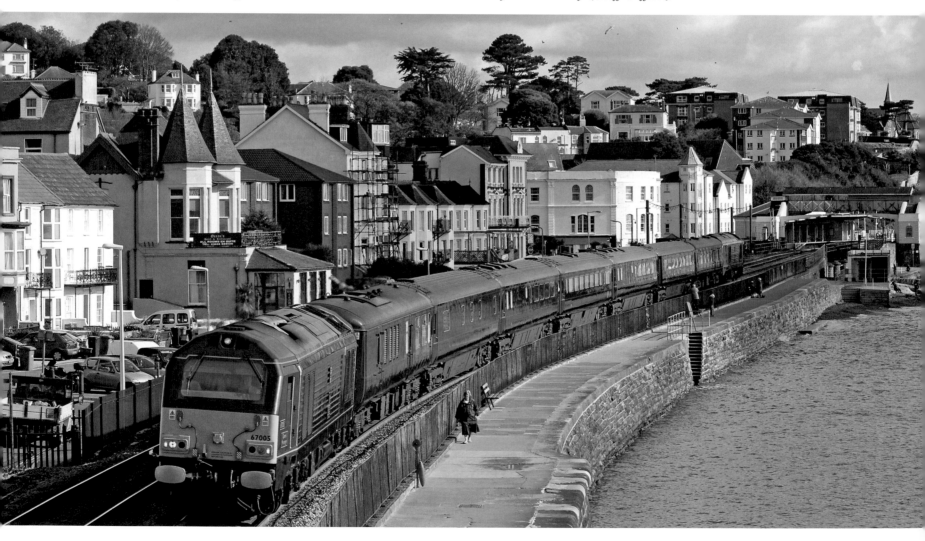

LEFT: *One of the busiest years for the Royal Train was 1977 when The Queen and Prince Philip made extensive use of it to tour the United Kingdom as part of the Silver Jubilee celebrations. Here, the Royal couple are bid farewell at Coventry by station manager Paul Caswell. (Patrick Kingston)*

BELOW: *It was a busy schedule again 25 years later for Her Majesty and His Royal Highness. This time the celebrations were to mark The Queen's Golden Jubilee in 2002. (Bob Sweet)*

by the Royal Family, and it does not follow that the same number of coaches are used every time. In the past it was even possible to see more than one Royal Train in different parts of the country on the same day. In fact, in 1986, three Royal Trains ran on the same day, although this was the only occasion when this has happened, and with the current number of carriages now available, it will never occur again – indeed, we shall not see more than one Royal Train operating at a time.

At present there are some nine coaches that can be assembled into whatever configuration is required, and for whom. There used to be 14, but this number was reduced in 1996, with two being retained as spares and the other three being sold on 31 March 2001 for £236,000, the proceeds going to the Department of Transport, Local Government and the Regions. Today, if The Queen and the Duke of Edinburgh are travelling together – and she rarely travels without him, although he does use the train when he is alone – then seven coaches are brought into operation.

Prince Charles is the most frequent and regular passenger. He also uses seven carriages. If the Duchess of Cornwall (not a lover of train travel, unlike her husband) accompanies him, as she often does on the long, overnight journeys to Scotland, then an extra carriage is attached for her use. This is usually one of

the Duke of Edinburgh's carriages, and is for the Duchess's staff, as her bedroom and sitting room are located in the same carriage as those of the Prince of Wales, but separated by a partition wall with a door between them. Occasionally, a five-coach train is used, but only for short journeys made in daytime when no sleeping car is required.

At present only four people are regular users of the Royal Train: The Queen, the Duke of Edinburgh, the Prince of Wales and the Duchess of Cornwall. Prince William and Prince Harry travel only if they are accompanying The Queen or the Prince of Wales, never alone, although of course, when Prince William becomes Prince of Wales, as Heir to the Throne, he will be entitled to use it. The Duke of York, the Earl of Wessex and the Princess Royal, who have all been frequent passengers in the past, no longer have the use of the train, partly on economic grounds, but also because helicopters are faster.

In April 1996 Prince Harry and Prince William journeyed from Slough to North Queensferry with their father, and diesel locomotive No 47799 *Prince Henry* pulled the train. The young Prince Harry climbed on board to inspect the locomotive, named after himself,

and was said to be slightly disappointed that it wasn't steam driven.

On 6 September 1997, both Prince William and Prince Harry, along with Earl Spencer, joined the Prince of Wales as they travelled from Euston to Long Buckby in Northamptonshire en route to Althorp where the interment of Princess Diana was to take place on the Spencer family estate. Appropriately, and sadly, The Train was powered by Nos 47798 *Prince William* and 47799 *Prince Henry* (see Chapter 7, 'Royal funeral trains').

The Royal Train is the only private, non-commercial train service, used by only one family, still in existence in the United Kingdom. However, to call it non-commercial is not strictly true as the Royal Family is charged the going rate for every mile they travel, and details of the expenditure are revealed in the annual accounts published by the Keeper of the Privy Purse (the Royal accountant), and are open to Government and public scrutiny every year.

In theory, Government departments are able to use the train for official business. In practice, so far the only occasion when a 'non-Royal' passenger has taken over the Royal Train was during the G8 Heads of Government

LEFT: *The Prince of Wales was on board as the Royal Train passed through Shrewsbury on 1 March 2006, St. David's Day. (Geoff Griffiths)*

DELOW. *Poulton le Fylde, Lancashire, on 11 April 2003 and the Royal Train is returning empty to Wolverton after conveying the Prince of Wales to an official visit to Blackpool. (Geoff Griffiths)*

Meeting in 1998. On 16 May that year, Cherie Blair, wife of the then Prime Minister, invited the wives of six of the world leaders to join her on a day trip from Birmingham to Little Kimble (the nearest station to Chequers, the Prime Minister's country residence in Buckinghamshire) and back. The ladies included Mrs Hillary Clinton, wife of the American President; Mrs Aline Chretien, whose husband was Canada's 20th Prime Minister; Signora Flavia Prodi of Italy; President Yeltsin of Russia's wife, Naina; Madame Bernadette Chirac of France; and from Japan, Mrs Kumiko Hashimoto. The ladies enjoyed a wonderful day out, with all the trimmings, in a seven-car Royal Train, hauled by the *Prince William* and *Prince Henry* locomotives.

They were waited on by the Royal stewards, with the best food and drink that could be asked for, and after the trip, Cherie Blair was photographed with several of the train crew, while Hillary Clinton gave the train foreman a signed and inscribed photograph of herself. Something that will, no doubt, become a collector's item in the future. It was during this journey that the Chief Steward on board played a little joke on the wife of Russia's President, telling her there was a problem with her hotel. She appeared slightly nonplussed and asked what she should do. He replied that she could go home with him and stay at his house for the night; his wife would be delighted. Mrs Yeltsin immediately brightened up and said that would be fine. Her reaction when she discovered it was all a joke has not been revealed.

It was also on this journey, when the train had been

hired by the Foreign and Commonwealth Office, that the VIPs had a bit of a shock. The train stopped for a moment at a station where they could hear a lot of noise coming from the platform. The net curtains were drawn back from the window in the saloon and they found themselves face to face with a crowd of red jersey-clad football fans who were on their way to the Cup Final (Arsenal beat Newcastle 2–0). The fans all wanted to see who was on board the Royal Train, and when the two sides suddenly saw each other neither was sure who suffered the greater shock. But it made a great story for the train crew.

British monarchs have favoured rail travel for more than 150 years. Queen Victoria became the first reigning sovereign to make a train journey when she travelled from Slough – at that time the nearest station to Windsor Castle – to Paddington, London, on 13 June 1842 (see Chapter 6, 'Early days'). However, while she may have been the first British *reigning* monarch to use this new form of transport, the Dowager Queen Adelaide, widow of King William IV, was the first *member* of the British Royal Family to make a train journey. This was two years earlier, on 22 July 1840, when she travelled from Nottingham to Leeds en route to staying at Harewood House and Bolton Abbey, by the North Midland Railway, in a train that consisted of three carriages and four trucks. The latter was for Her Majesty's entourage.

This journey was notable also for the fact that it was the first time that a sleeping compartment had been installed in a train. It was not all that comfortable by modern standards, of course, but the décor was elaborate and the brass bedstead and feather bed were

considered to be eminently suitable for Royalty to rest on. The coaches were decorated with white figured satin linings and trimmings and sarsenet blinds. The exterior had been ornamented with gilt and the springs were the same as those used by the company on their mail carriages. The train speed was limited to 30mph, so there was not too much chance of a rocky ride and apparently Her Majesty made no complaints.

The history of Royalty and railways is steeped in time-honoured tradition, since Queen Adelaide made that first journey, and successive kings, queens, princes and princesses have continued to become inveterate rail travellers.

If it had not been for those early Royal passengers, a doubtful public would not have been so quickly persuaded that trains were a safe, comfortable and efficient means of transport. The development of trains in the middle of the 19th century meant that a previously sceptical public not only saw the advantages of rail travel as a convenient way to get from place to place, but it also soon became extremely fashionable.

In 1869 Queen Victoria, by then a seasoned rail traveller, commissioned a special pair of coaches which she paid for with the assistance of the LNWR, at a cost of £1,800 – a considerable sum in those days. Her Majesty remains to this day the only sovereign to have actually paid with her own money for Royal saloons to be built.

When her son succeeded to the throne as King Edward VII, he ordered a completely new Royal Train in the second year of his reign, 1902, with the instructions that 'it is to be as much like the Royal Yacht as possible.'

The interior had every modern facility: bedrooms, dressing rooms, day rooms and a smoking room. It boasted three-speed electric fans, electric radiators and cookers and even an electric cigar lighter. The King's favourite saloon was his smoking room that was manned by two liveried footmen, one just to light His Majesty's cigars and the other to adjust the curtains and windows in case the sunlight was too strong or fresh air was required.

Successive monarchs from Victoria to Elizabeth II have all enjoyed trains and used them to carry out the business of monarchy. Edward VII made great use of his Royal Train and took personal interest in the design and

ABOVE: *As the Royal Train passed through Bawtry, Nottinghamshire, on 4 July 2007, its passengers and crew were able to see at first hand the effect of the massive flooding in the area. (Geoff Griffiths)*

OPPOSITE: *The Royal Train, with locomotive No. 67005, standing at Doncaster, one of the rail network's most famous railway towns. The Royal passenger was Prince Charles, travelling from York to Andover. (Geoff Griffiths)*

decoration of his carriages, while his son and heir, as King George V, had the distinction of installing the first bath on a train anywhere in the world. He did this in 1915, during the First World War, when he and Queen Mary made many extensive tours of Britain to boost morale. Due to the severe wartime restrictions, which the King insisted on observing for himself and his family, he felt it would be unfair to expect his traditional hosts throughout the country – the aristocracy – to offer their usual lavish hospitality, so he and the Queen chose to remain on board the train overnight, hence the need for a bath. But it was minute by any standards, measuring just 55in long by 25in wide. Queen Mary, very sensibly, would only use it while the train was standing still, but

the King had no such qualms. George V also installed the first radio in the Royal Train when he was persuaded to allow one to be used in his sitting room in 1935. Of course, history has recorded that His Majesty was also the first British sovereign to make a Christmas broadcast on the wireless.

The bath he installed in 1915 continued to be used throughout the remainder of George V's reign, until he died in 1936, then his son David enjoyed its unique facilities – but only once – during his brief reign as Edward VIII. When his brother Albert succeeded him as King George VI after the Abdication, he also made use of the bath on wheels for another five years, particularly during the first two years of the Second World War, until

ABOVE: *HRH The Duchess of Cornwall made her first journey on the Royal Train on 13 July 2005; here she is seen disembarking at Machynlleth. (Geoff Griffiths)*

a more modern, full-sized bath was installed in 1941.

An all-too-common misconception about the Royal Train is that, just because it has the word 'Royal' attached to it, it must follow that it is the last word in luxury. It is not. No one would deny that the train is extremely comfortable, with an air of country house 'old money' about it, but the present author has seen a number of private rail coaches in other countries, such as the United States, that make the British Royal Train seem positively Spartan by comparison. Even today there are private trains running in India that are truly Palaces on Wheels and these are operated solely for their owner's pleasure, whereas in Britain, the Royal Train is functional and economical, there purely to transport The Queen and her family throughout the realm on official business.

The most recent addition to luxury trains in India is the 'Golden Chariot', built at a cost of £7 million and which contains a fully equipped gymnasium, two massage rooms and every cabin is en suite and fitted with hand-woven bed coverings, silk sheets, DVDs and plasma television sets. The train is also equipped with a special, 35-seat conference coach – but, strangely, no swimming pool! So the British Royal Train still has some way to go.

In the latter part of the 19th century and throughout the 20th, all the major railway companies operating in the British Isles owned railway carriages that were dedicated for use by the Royal Family. As recently as 1948, when the railway system was nationalised and formed into British Railways, the different regions continued to maintain and operate their own individual Royal Train coaches, each one trying to outdo the others in splendour and comfort.

The first recent major milestone for Royal rail travel occurred in 1977, the year of The Queen's Silver Jubilee. Her Majesty and the Duke of Edinburgh planned an extensive tour of the United Kingdom and, as a result, a single set of 'Royal Train' carriages was formed and has remained in service ever since, even surviving the re-privatisation of the railways in 1996.

Just because a Royal Train exists and is used exclusively by the Royal Family, it does not follow that every time they travel by rail they use the 'Train'. The Princess Royal frequently joins other passengers on 'ordinary' scheduled services when she travels between her home in Gloucestershire and London, without any fuss or any special arrangements being made for her.

Before the Princess is expected, a manager is dispatched from First Great Western HQ at Swindon to check the state of the carriage she will occupy. He makes sure that previous occupants have not left any debris on the seats or under the table, the seat reservations are in place, and the train manager and trolley attendant are aware that they have a Royal passenger. He travels on every journey but makes himself 'invisible' to the Princess as she hates being overcrowded. There is no 'meet and greet' party on departure or arrival (on her express wish), but he does keep in contact with his office at HQ so he can let Her Royal Highness know if there is going to be any delay.

The other passengers in the carriage are usually aware of who they are travelling with, but there is little fuss and nobody is excluded from passing through. Although six seats are reserved, only one has to be paid for by the Palace and that is for the Princess herself – even so, it is bought at a discount because, as the wife of a serving

LEFT: *In his role as the Duke of Cornwall, Prince Charles travels another spectacular route, alongside the sea at Teignmouth, Devon, on 8 May 2003. (Geoff Griffiths)*

RIGHT: *The Prince of Wales held a small dinner party on 7 June 2007 on board the Royal Train, which ran from Bangor to Holyhead, reversed and then proceeded back to Bangor, via Valley (on the Isle of Anglesey) to allow the dinner to be served. (Geoff Griffiths)*

Royal Navy officer, she carries a Forces Family Railcard.

First-class passengers on a recent train from London to York were agreeably surprised to find the Duchess of Cornwall sitting quietly among them, with only her police officer for company and a man from EWS sitting opposite. The Duchess even accepted a cup of tea and a biscuit from the catering assistant when the trolley came around, and didn't object too strenuously when a couple of fellow passengers used their mobile video phones to take her photograph.

The days when a top-hatted, frock-coated stationmaster was always in attendance at every Royal departure and arrival have long since disappeared, except occasionally when The Queen is the expected passenger.

When The Queen had the use of the Royal Yacht, there was always an Admiral in command (until the Government of the day decided in their wisdom to downgrade the post to that of a Commodore during the final years of *Britannia*'s service). Similarly, Her Majesty's personal 'airline', The Queen's Flight, had a Royal Air Force officer, invariably an Air Vice Marshal, as Captain of The Queen's Flight, with responsibility for all Royal flying. That rank also was reduced when The Queen's Flight was disbanded and merged with No 32 Squadron (the Royal Flight) on 1 April 1995. The squadron is not restricted to use by the Royal Family and is often used by Government ministers.

Perhaps strangely, there has never been a 'Royal Train Driver' as such. No one man has been singled out and honoured as The Queen's personal engine driver. There is a small pool of very senior and experienced drivers always available and the theory is that when one is required for Royal duties, the next man on the roster gets the job. That is the theory, but perhaps it is not too surprising that when one looks at the roster, the same names appear time and time again. Of course, it is well known that The Queen and other members of the Royal Family like to see familiar faces around them and whenever possible they prefer not to have strangers looking after them.

The vehicles that make up the Royal Train are based at Wolverton in Buckinghamshire when not in use. They are under the control of a railway special vehicles manager, who liaises with the Director of Royal Travel at Buckingham Palace, as well as his colleagues at the other railway organisations involved in Royal journeys. The Director has overall responsibility for organising not only all rail journeys for Royalty, but also all flights, sea voyages and, together with the Crown Equerry, requirements for cars and limousines.

As with anything to do with the Royal Family, rail journeys are usually planned many months in advance, or even, as was the case during Silver Jubilee year, 1977, well over a year before. Even Royal funeral arrangements, such as that of the late Earl Mountbatten of Burma, are worked out down to the smallest detail if they involve a rail journey. Lord Mountbatten took a personal interest in his own funeral arrangements and had even chosen the menu for the meals to be eaten by those accompanying his coffin from London to Romsey in Hampshire, where he was finally laid to rest. It says much for Lord Mountbatten's attention to detail that on the day of his funeral, coffee was just being finished as the Royal Train pulled into Romsey station.

Any individual rail trip by Royalty involves the efforts of hundreds of men and women from every part of the proposed route. Engineers and technicians check and double check the locomotives that will power the train – there is always a spare – while the cleaners, upholsterers and painters who regularly service and maintain the Royal and Household saloons, make sure everything is in pristine condition.

An engineering car is attached to the train for every journey and there is a back-up power unit to provide all the electrical requirements.

If the train is stationary overnight, it will be positioned in a secluded siding well away from the main line. The location of these sidings, which are sited throughout the country, is restricted to a very few people on a strictly 'need to know' basis.

The Queen's saloon is fitted with double doors that open on her arrival at her destination so that she can emerge gracefully onto the

BELOW: *EWS Class 67 No. 67029* **Royal Diamond** *in silver livery, at Slindon, Staffordshire, on 24 October 2007. This is an empty stock working from Wolverton to Ayr to pick up the Prince of Wales and the Duchess of Cornwall to bring them back to London.* (Geoff Griffiths)

BELOW: *A good night's sleep could be guaranteed in this snug sleeping car, with its comfortable fittings and scenic photographs on the walls. (Railcare)*

platform. Prince Charles enjoys the same privilege, and he does have another distinction: he insists on taking his own travelling crockery and cutlery sets on the train. However, Charles, along with all his family – including his parents – does eat and drink the food and wine offered by the rail company Rail Gourmet. The Royal chef does not normally cook on board, but nevertheless the meals are of superlative quality, even if comparatively simple by Palace standards, and The Queen has been served by the same senior railway steward for more than twenty years (see Chapter 2, 'Royal meals on railway wheels').

The present Royal Family has few extraordinary culinary demands, unlike some previous monarchs such as King Edward VII who preferred to eat food that had been shot, caught or trapped on his own estates. Or Queen Victoria, who believed it was 'unnatural' and harmful to the digestion to eat anything while on the move. While hers was the first train in the world to have a lavatory installed on board, only the Prince Consort used it in the early days of Royal progress. So the poor members of the entourage who invariably accompanied the Queen, had to wait until the train

stopped before being allowed to 'spend a penny'. Hence the elaborate refreshment rooms that were built for the use of Queen Victoria and her Household at various stations all along the route from Windsor to Ballater, the nearest station to Balmoral. Sadly, many of these stations have long been closed, along with the rail tracks that served them, but volunteer enthusiasts have, in some cases, maintained these refreshment rooms as living museums commemorating a gracious and bygone age of Royal travel.

So, in an age when air travel by jet-propelled aircraft is taken for granted and it is possible for anyone to cross to the other side of the world in a matter of hours, it is refreshing to learn that The Queen and her family still prefer the more leisurely, dignified and infinitely more civilised pleasure of travelling by train – even if it is no longer the 'Age of Steam'.

In the pages that follow, the author explains the intricacies of Royal travel by rail and the way in which, by using the railway network, without disrupting scheduled services, The Queen and her family are able to carry out their official engagements in a speedy, economic and efficient manner.

ABOVE: *The Prince of Wales's sitting room, with its chintz-covered sofa and armchairs, reflects the Royal Family's preference for 'country-house' comfort, rather than ostentatious luxury. (RAIL magazine)*

CHAPTER 1

The Train now standing at Platform...

O N THURSDAY, 6 March 2008 The Queen had no
official engagements listed in the Court Circular,
but she did have a full programme of duties at
Buckingham Palace, while the Duke of Edinburgh had a
reception to attend in the evening. His Royal Highness
spent a couple of hours meeting guests and chatting,
without giving the slightest hint that he was anxious to
leave and get ready for an overnight trip to Wales.

Arriving back in his quarters, he was met by one of his
two valets who had laid out a change of clothes; the
Duke does not select what he is going to wear, he says
that is what he pays his valets to do. They had already
been given a copy of the next day's programme, so they
knew the correct suits to pack and, sometimes even
more importantly, the right ties. If His Royal Highness is
meeting several different organisations or service units
with which he is associated, he always wears their tie,
sometimes changing up to five times a day. For the
journey to Wales, one of the valets would be

LEFT: *A full-length view of the Royal Train with the Prince of
Wales on board as it approaches Tal-y-Cafn in North Wales
on 25 April 2008, top-and-tailed by the pair of Royal
locomotives, Nos 67005 and 67006. (Geoff Griffiths)*

accompanying Prince Philip while the other travelled to Windsor Castle to await HRH's return the next day.

After a light dinner in the private apartments at Buckingham Palace, The Queen and the Duke of Edinburgh left the Garden Entrance to the Palace (that's the one on the extreme right as you look at the building from the front) and entered one of the Royal cars to travel to London's Euston station, where the Royal Train was waiting for them.

The motorcade – with police outriders and a back-up vehicle – drove straight into the station and on to the platform where the Royal Train was waiting, and the moment Her Majesty and His Royal Highness were on board and settled in their saloon, the train departed for Swansea, where the following day there was a full programme of engagements. It was exactly 23.04, the time scheduled more than a month earlier.

Nick Edwards, the Royal Train Officer, had been involved in the arrangements for this journey for many weeks. His qualifications for the job are impressive as he has been Traction Inspector for the Train in the past and he was also the youngest person ever to take the controls of the Royal Train when, at 21 years of age, he first drove the Prince of Wales.

Working in close collaboration with Chris Hillyard, the Train Foreman, and Geoff Griffiths, EWS Royal Train Account Manager, he knows exactly what needs to be done before every Royal journey. The tasks include choosing the men who are going to drive the train. EWS (English Welsh & Scottish Railway) employs some 1,800 drivers, from whom they have a pool of around 150 who are Class One competent, which means they are able to drive Royal Trains. In practice though, the selection is restricted to about 50 men who have control regularly.

On this particular journey, five drivers were scheduled to be in charge of the locomotives: one each from the depots at Bescot (Birmingham), Wembley, Margam, Newport and Bristol. The back-up crew included a

BELOW: *Wolverton has been home to the Royal Train for over 150 years and this is where the coaches are prepared and serviced before all Royal journeys. (RAIL magazine)*

Traction Inspector and Locomotive Technical Rider from EWS, a Network Rail Inspector, two of Chris Hillyard's staff at Wolverton, who accompanied him (he travels on every Royal journey), three catering staff: the Chief Steward, Ken Moule, his colleagues Bob Bigsby, David Holt and Chef Martin Carter, and the ever-present British Transport Police officer.

Before the train left Wolverton, Chris Hillyard's team cleaned and prepared the exterior and interior of the coaches, paying particular attention to the placement of HM's and HRH's personal effects and proving all the on-board systems: security, heating and air conditioning, the water supply and the communications systems. This is undertaken before every journey and once Chris is satisfied, the Royal saloons and Household coaches are pulled out of the shed and assembled into the correct configuration by a Railcare shunting engine, with the power car at the front and the escort car on the rear. There are two catering vehicles, one each for the Royal party and the accompanying Household.

At this point it effectively becomes the Royal Train operated by EWS and managed by Nick Edwards, who adds the two locomotives that are going to haul the train. On this occasion they are Nos 67005 *Queen's Messenger* and 67006 *Royal Sovereign*. Thereafter the final mandatory brake tests are undertaken on both the engines and the coaches, and the head and tail lights checked to make sure the train is fit for purpose when

ABOVE: *The Royal Train heads back to London in 2008 with one of the Spanish-built Class 67s in charge. (Geoff Griffiths)*

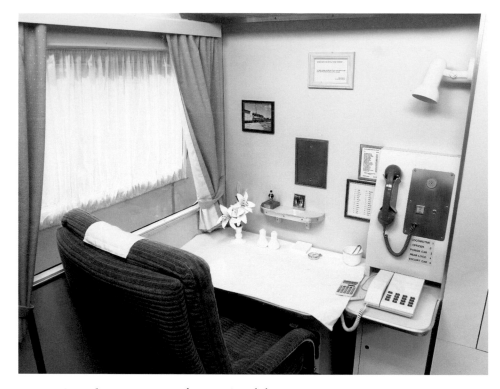

ABOVE: *From the moment the Royal Train leaves its base at Wolverton until it returns, it is the responsibility of the Train Officer, Nick Edwards. This is his personal office on board, from where he controls and monitors the journeys and maintains contact with his colleagues. (RAIL magazine)*

OPPOSITE: *Prince Charles gave a business luncheon on board the Train as it ran from Llandudno Junction to Prestatyn and Shotton in 2008. HRH often uses the Royal Train for meetings and small business conferences as it can be much more convenient than bringing lots of people to London. (Geoff Griffiths)*

the appointed departure time arrives.

The Train Officer also has to liaise with Network Control at this point, telling them the various mobile telephone numbers they might need during the journey. He checks his own contingency arrangements just in case there is a need to change plans for any reason, as there was on the overnight journey of 21/23 January 2008. The Royal Train had been despatched from Wolverton to collect the Prince of Wales from Ayr and bring him to Malton the following day. The weather had been appalling and conditions were among the worst the Train Officer and his operational team had ever encountered. They were going up the West Coast route to Scotland when they came up against severe flooding north of Preston.

Nick Edwards had to make a decision, either to divert from his scheduled route or try to continue. At 4pm that afternoon he decided at Carlisle to head north east towards Edinburgh and managed to find a line that was open to Ayr. Picking up Prince Charles as intended, the train then travelled south through York and Scarborough and His Royal Highness was able to leave the train at Malton exactly on time. Later, they continued with him on board to King's Lynn in Norfolk so that Prince Charles could then journey by car to Sandringham. This was a typical problem that the Royal Train Officer has to

solve and whenever the train is due to be used in the winter, he knows the weather can be unpredictable, so alternative routes are always investigated.

Back to this current journey, communications are established with the onboard engineer, the traction inspector accompanying the driver in his cab via a radio link so that, should the need arise, Network Control can contact the train direct. The radio system on the train has been using the same alpha/numeric code for many years. The lead locomotive is Grove 1, the Train Officer is Grove 2, Network Rail is Grove 3, and the rear engine is Grove 4. The word 'Grove' goes back to the days when the headquarters of the old London, Midland & Scottish Railway was at Grove House, Watford, during the Second World War.

By now all the staff who will be working the train are on board and the final checks have been completed and watches synchronised. They all have to check their watches and clocks against the Train Officer's time, who has set his watch by the speaking clock, and that's the one they will work with until they leave the train the next day. The train then departs from Wolverton for Euston station to await the arrival of the Royal party.

Because the Royal Train uses the same platform so frequently there are permanent marks to enable the driver to see exactly where he should bring it to a halt. There is a red mark on one of the overhead gantries and a white mark on the platform which lines up with the guard's door. From years of practice, the drivers know just where to bring the train in, and at what speed.

The train has been brought into Euston at least half an hour before the scheduled departure time in order for the Royal Household support staff and the luggage to be loaded and unpacked before the principals arrive. Once they are on board, the train waits for no one. The Queen's private secretary, or one of the assistants, always accompanies her on Royal Train journeys as Her Majesty will spend part of the journey working on her 'boxes'. These are the red cases that go with her wherever she is anywhere in the world, containing official documents, letters and communications from Government departments, both in the United Kingdom and the Commonwealth, that have to be read and initialled by Her Majesty before they can become approved.

ABOVE AND LEFT: *The ritual when The Queen arrives never varies. She is always greeted by the Lord Lieutenant (her own representative) of the county she is visiting. On this occasion, Her Majesty is at Manchester Victoria station where, in addition to the Lord Lieutenant, a crowd of well-wishers has gathered to welcome her and offer bouquets of flowers. (Geoff Griffiths)*

The Queen's senior dresser, who is also now her personal assistant, is on board, having laid out Her Majesty's night clothes and prepared the wardrobe for the following day's engagements. The Travelling Yeoman, a senior footman, was among the first members of the Royal Household to join the train – he is responsible for the luggage belonging to all the Royal party, including the Household, and he makes sure the cases are all placed in the correct coaches.

Representatives of EWS and the Network Rail duty station manager at Euston form the small reception committee when Her Majesty and His Royal Highness arrive, but there is little ceremony. This is a formality that has been gone through many times before and the

BELOW: *Although this is a formality Her Majesty has gone through many times before, she always manages to make it appear that she still enjoys these occasions as much as if they were her first. Here she is greeted by the Lord Lieutenant of Cumbria at Whitehaven on 5 June 2008. (Geoff Griffiths)*

railway staff all know that The Queen does not like any fuss; she just wants to board the train as quickly as possible, and Chris Hillyard undertakes to lift the step and close the doors once all passengers have entrained. Chris, in smart black blazer and grey trousers, is wearing his RVM, awarded by The Queen for personal services to the Royal Family.

Her Majesty's personal assistant and senior dresser is standing by in the Royal saloon and, as this is a night-time departure, The Queen will be offered light refreshments of warm sausage rolls, smoked salmon, chicken or egg sandwiches, made with brown and white bread – all with the crusts removed – and may drink a glass of still water. This is provided by Chief Steward, Ken Moule who, with the other stewards, is wearing his regulation uniform of charcoal grey suit complete with the miniature decorations for which he is eligible, white

shirt and highly polished black shoes. All the railway crew are also wearing the distinctive Royal Train tie, either navy blue or burgundy with a gold stripe and bearing a crown with the initials RT below. The tie shows that they belong to a most exclusive club – but they have to pay for this out of their own pockets, it is not given to them.

Once all is ready, the Train Officer makes his final rounds to check that all the doors are locked, and informs the police that they are about to leave. Network Rail (Grove 3) are contacted to make sure the signal to depart is set at green and the Traction Inspector and driver are aware of the speed that has been set for them. This is always lower than the normal maximum; so if crossing a set of points is usually restricted to 20mph, the Royal Train will cross at 15mph, in order to make it a smoother ride.

The Train Officer sets up his 'headquarters' in the power car with his laptop, GPS, mobile phone and radio set. He has a tiny bedroom in the adjacent sleeping car, with office facilities and wardrobe, and there he will remain during the rest of the journey. He is in contact with his colleagues in the escort car and none of the occupants will venture further than the next coach once the principals are on board, unless there is an urgent reason.

The train leaves Euston and moves slowly across London to join the westbound line just outside Paddington Station. By the time it reaches that point the last passenger train of the day has departed so there is a clear run all the way through the Severn Tunnel to Wales.

As the Royal Train coaches do not all have corridors, it is impossible to get from one end to the other without going through the Royal saloons, so when The Queen and her family are on board, only those people who have to see them (members of the Household and the train stewards) are allowed into the Royal sections. When the train reached the overnight 'stabling' point, near Port Talbot in South Wales, it was secured for the night. The local police were informed and the engines closed down with the battery switches taken out, because obviously the operators would not want the embarrassment of flat batteries when they came to start

up again the next morning. The train was equipped with an independent air supply from a small compressor in the power car supplying the requirements throughout the train during the stop. There was a flurry of behind-the-scenes activities and Nick Edwards knew he would not be getting very much sleep that night, an hour or so if he was lucky.

At 5 o'clock on Friday morning the train came alive again – quietly so as not to wake the principals or the Household staff travelling with them – as the crew prepared for the final run into Swansea. Phil George, an experienced driver from Margam, whose day began around 3.30am, came to take over for the last few miles. Mr George, wearing his best uniform, has been driving trains since 1981 and has driven the Royal Train at least half a dozen times. He explained that he gets four days notice when a 'Special Train' is to be driven but he is not told it is the Royal Train. However, with his years of

experience he says It doesn't take a genius to know what is going on. The day before he joined this journey Phil was driving a freight train pulling steel wagons, the day before that an oil train, and a few weeks previously he had charge of a football excursion. As he put it: 'Variety is the spice of life.'

The Queen and the Duke of Edinburgh are woken at 7.30 with the 'calling trays': tea for Her Majesty, coffee for His Royal Highness as he only drinks tea in the afternoon. They meet to have breakfast together in Her Majesty's sitting room, with its small table that can seat four, but they are never joined by any members of their Household at breakfast. It is one of the few times in the day when they will be truly alone and they treasure the moments when they can chat about private matters and perhaps discuss the engagements that lie ahead.

Ken Moule waits on them and The Queen always enjoys the same breakfast when she is on board:

ABOVE: *The Royal Train passing the signalbox at Llanrwst in North Wales in 2008, with the Prince of Wales on board. (Geoff Griffiths)*

OPPOSITE: *Two of the Royal Train's most important 'non-Royal' personnel: Angela Kelly, The Queen's personal assistant and arguably the person closer to Her Majesty than anyone else outside the Royal Family, and Chris Hillyard, Special Vehicles Manager and Royal Train Foreman, who travels on every journey. (Mick Foster)*

scrambled eggs and bacon, prepared by Chef Martin Carter, who knows exactly how she and the Duke like their food. Her Majesty doesn't always clear her plate as she is not a big eater. All the morning newspapers, tabloids and broadsheets, have been delivered to the train and one of the private secretaries has marked anything he thinks might be of particular interest. The one newspaper no one ever touches is *The Racing Post*, the 'bible' of the racing fraternity that is required reading at the Royal breakfast table every morning, no matter where The Queen is. In Britain it is delivered by hand; abroad it is electronically transmitted to Her Majesty. Without this, it is said, she would suffer severe 'withdrawal symptoms'!

By the time breakfast is ended and the principals – and the Royal Household in their dining car – have all had their first meal of the day, the crew are making ready to move. The Queen's dresser is on hand helping Her Majesty with her outfit for the day.

The engine is started at least half an hour before they are due to leave, just in case there are any problems; on this occasion there were none. Once Nick Edwards was satisfied that everything was as it should be and the principals were happy to move, he called Network Rail to let them know they were about to get under way. For this critical part of the journey, as the train had to arrive dead on time, Nick moved into the locomotive cab alongside the Traction Inspector and Phil George the locomotive driver.

It is a point of honour for all the Royal Train drivers not to cause any jolting and to make all departures and arrivals so smooth that the passengers would hardly know the train was moving. So, once the signal to leave had been given, it was notch one, release the brake and gradually increase speed until they reached the required speed to get them to Swansea at exactly the time they were scheduled. At this point the Train Officer is merely observing, leaving the operation in the capable hands of the driver and Traction Inspector. They have been given a written timetable showing just where they should be at any given time, and cover the distance from Port Talbot to Swansea at a leisurely 40mph, noting that they are passing the relevant checkpoints at the correct time and adjusting their speed accordingly. The aim is to be at the

LEFT: Seen passing Abergele & Pensarn signalbox – a popular spot for railway photographers – in 2008, the Royal Train was conveying the Prince of Wales from Euston to Tal-y-Cafn. (Geoff Griffiths)

approach end of Platform 1 at Swansea High Street station with 90 seconds to go so that they can glide smoothly to a halt, dead on time. It works; somehow it always does.

As Phil George, sitting at the controls of the *Queen's Messenger*, brings it majestically and almost silently into the station, a railway colleague is standing at the far end of the platform holding a yellow flag at arm's length. This is to show Phil exactly where he has to bring his cab to a halt so that The Queen's double doors will open at the precise spot where the welcoming party is waiting. He stops the engine inch perfect and switches off, but he is not allowed to leave the cab, or even look out of the window, until the Royal Party has departed. Nick Edwards can be proud of his planning and execution, as the Royal Train has arrived within five seconds of the appointed time: 10.02am.

The Royal couple descend the steps on to the platform at Swansea with the door being attended by Chris Hillyard, who gives a short neck bow as they pass. The Queen is wearing a fawn-coloured coat and matching hat while the Duke is in a light grey lounge suit. Waiting to greet them are the Lord Lieutenant of Mid-Glamorgan and the Lord Mayor of Swansea, plus a representative of EWS. A small group of well-wishers has been allowed onto the platform, including several in wheelchairs. The Queen and the Duke spend a few minutes chatting with them before they leave by car for first engagement of the morning.

On this occasion The Queen and the Duke are not returning by train, but flying back from Swansea airport,

so there is a sense of relaxation on board as the crew prepare to leave Swansea for Wolverton. Phil George climbs down from his cab and walks the length of the train to get back on board as the train will be in reverse: this time it is *Royal Sovereign* he is driving. It takes him only a couple of minutes to get the locomotive started and away they go, just one minute before the next London train, standing at an adjoining platform, is due to leave.

As the Royal Train does not have to make any stops until nearer its destination it will stay in front to avoid interfering with the scheduled service. Some members of the Royal Household are travelling back with them part of the way, being dropped en route to Windsor, and they all feel it has gone very well. Nick Edwards, Chris Hillyard and their colleagues settle down to a full English breakfast in comfort as the train speeds along the route out of Wales – until the next time. But there is still one final chore for them all. The Train Officer, Train Foreman, Traction Inspector and British Transport Police each have to write and file a detailed report on the journey, up to eight pages long – and hope there will be no adverse comments from the Royal Family.

They all have funny incidents to tell about things that happened in the past, but thankfully, not this time. There was one occasion when the train was travelling to collect the Prince of Wales and made a brief unscheduled stop at a station platform. No-one noticed a middle-aged lady get on (there is no central locking on the Royal Train) – the first anyone realised there was an 'unauthorised' passenger on board was when one of the crew walked through the Household dining car and saw this lady calmly sitting there at one of the tables. He reported back to the Train Officer who then went and asked how and when she had got on. When he explained that this was the Royal Train, she was

The Queen's Corgi dogs are a familiar sight on the Royal Train but on at least one occasion they have given the staff something of a fright. (Getty images)

completely unfazed and said she would get off at the next stop. It was pointed out that the next stop was in fact a station siding close to where the Prince of Wales would be joining the train, and she would have to remain on board until then. Eventually, Ken Moule donned his best uniform and served her the obligatory 'light refreshments', compliments of the Royal Train. When they arrived at the scheduled siding, she was courteously escorted from the train, and put on the appropriate platform for a train to where she wanted to go in the first place, none the worse for her adventure. It certainly gave her something to tell friends at the next meeting of her local Women's Institute.

The only occasion when anyone can remember the train failing to stop at the correct point was on 1 April 1999. The Queen and Prince Philip were travelling overnight from Euston to Bristol for the annual Maundy Service. For some reason the train planning did not work out quite as they thought and the train arrived at Bristol Temple Meads station the opposite way round from that expected. The result was that the Principals' door was now six coaches away from where the local dignitaries were waiting.

Her Majesty and His Royal Highness noticed that the

reception party was being left in their wake as the train slowly drew to a halt and they witnessed a very distressed Lord Lieutenant, in full uniform, complete with ceremonial sword dangling between his legs, hurrying up the platform, desperately trying to maintain a sense of dignity. The Duke of Edinburgh suggested, tongue in cheek, that 'a cock-up's been made' – something of an understatement judging by the expression on the poor old Lord Lieutenant's face. To which Ken Moule uttered the immortal phrase: 'Well, it is April Fool's Day Sir.' At that point everyone, Her Majesty, His Royal Highness and their senior Household, collapsed into hysterics (out of sight of the reception party), and thus any potential complaint that was expected, never materialised.

During the years when Chris Hillyard was working as Royal Train electrician, he was involved in an incident with The Queen at night. They were travelling between Aberdeen and London, following the Royal Family's annual holiday at Balmoral. Shortly after leaving Aberdeen Chris was informed that all radio communication between the train and the outside world had been lost and he was ordered to attend to the repairs. This meant he had to go through the Royal apartments, and on being advised that both Principals had retired for the night, he was satisfied that he could pass through without disturbing them.

However, Chris had not been told that on this occasion The Queen had brought her nine Corgi dogs with her, so when he opened the door to the saloon, imagine his shock at finding 18 little green eyes staring at him. Quickly closing the door again he memorised the route across the floor that would not entail him stepping on the animals. He again entered the saloon in the dark and just as he was reaching the door handle at the far side of the room, the door opened and he

| *The Royal Train*

stood face to face with The Queen. Neither moved for a second and it was difficult to say which was the more surprised. Chris apologised to Her Majesty, who said she understood and that she was just checking her 'charges', prior to retiring for the night. She then switched the lights on and, of course, the Corgis made a dash for her. Unfortunately, Chris was standing between them and their mistress and it took a few minutes to disentangle the mêlée. Once calm had been restored, Chris apologised again and prepared to leave. As he did so, Her Majesty sweetly enquired if he intended returning through the train later. He said he would not and indeed, waited more than two hours and many miles further into the journey, before returning to his post, by walking along the platform at the next station. Shaken but not stirred!

The Queen and the Duke of Edinburgh travelled to Southampton on 6 April 1995 where Her Majesty was to name the new P&O liner *Oriana*. On the return journey to Slough, The Queen's saloon suddenly filled with smoke and Chris Hillyard was summoned to investigate. He discovered a 'dragging brake' was the cause of the trouble and the air-conditioning unit was drawing in the smoke. The train was stopped immediately, as was all traffic on the adjacent lines. Chris, dressed in full Royal Train livery, jumped down on to the track to make the necessary adjustments, watched throughout by Her Majesty, who was very interested in what was happening and effectively acted as a volunteer look-out during the repairs. Surely the first, and only, time the monarch has been recruited as 'assistant' to a railway worker?

In 2002, Golden Jubilee Year, the Royal Train was used extensively. On 7 May, when the train arrived at Sunderland, it naturally stopped at the correct spot for The Queen and the Duke to detrain. Unfortunately, the locomotive's exhaust was directly under a smoke detector (which should have been isolated) and all the station's alarms were activated, much to the dismay of the dignitaries waiting to greet the Royal couple. However, The Queen and the Duke calmly proceeded to go through the motions as if this was an everyday occurrence and nothing out of the ordinary had happened, while all around them panic ensued.

These unusual incidents are never reported in the press, but they are all recorded in the reports compiled by the train operators after each journey – and to the outsider, they make fascinating reading.

LEFT: *The Queen and the Duke of Edinburgh travelled to Southampton East Docks on 6 April 1995 where Her Majesty named the new P&O liner* **Oriana**, *which is seen with the Royal Train alongside, with Class 47 No. 47739* **Resourceful** *at the head. It was on the return journey to Slough that The Queen's saloon suddenly filled with smoke, which turned out to be a 'dragging brake' and the problem was quickly resolved. (Mick Foster)*

CHAPTER 2

Royal meals on railway wheels

W HEN THE QUEEN and other members of the Royal Family join the Royal Train all the arrangements are in place to make their journey as comfortable as possible. From aperitifs to fine dining or just plain wholesome food, the person who makes sure all the right ingredients are on board the Train is Roger Williams. He is the Catering Manager of the Royal Train employed by Rail Gourmet, which is a subsidiary of the world's leading food travel company SSP. It is his job to make sure the right supplies are ordered for each journey and that they are delivered to the train on time – all of which is accounted for through the catering contract Rail Gourmet has with EWS.

The Royal Train is only a tiny part of the Rail Gourmet and SSP business, with a catering cost of only around £25,000 a year, out of a total of £1.3 billion turnover for the company as a whole. But for this special operation, contracts are not the issue for Roger and his Rail Gourmet team – it's the pride they take in their unique roles that makes it all work so smoothly.

RIGHT: *The Queen's Golden Jubilee year, 2002, was one of the busiest for the Royal Train in recent times. This is No. 6233* **Duchess of Sutherland,** *at Bangor, North Wales, in June of that year. (Geoff Griffiths)*

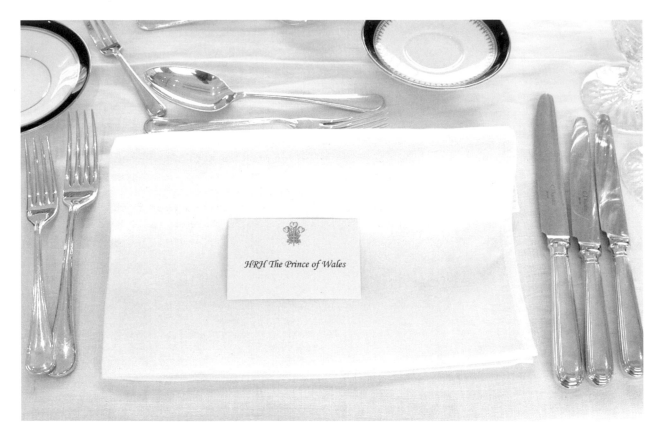

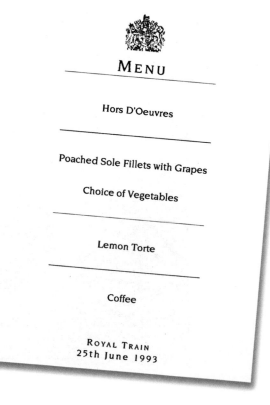

If The Queen wants afternoon tea with toasted teacake or an aperitif (her favourite is one-third gin, two-thirds Dubonnet and lots of ice), if the Duke of Edinburgh wants a glass of Double Diamond beer or kippers for breakfast, or the Prince of Wales asks for a Welsh rarebit made with his own organic cheese, the team will respond and in many cases probably be able to anticipate what is required and how it should be served. The main supply of food and drink is made possible through the purchasing and product delivery systems of Rail Gourmet, although there are some occasions when special food supplies are sent direct from the Palace.

Behind the scenes, however, it has not always been that easy to keep the service going. Roger Williams explains: 'When the railway was privatised in the 1990s we saw British Rail split into some 25 new commercial companies, none of whom was particularly interested in continuing to operate the Train as there was very little money in it. The Board had to be convinced that we should cater for the Train on a 'cost-only' basis without making any profit, whilst we also had to demonstrate to the Royal Travel Office that we were able to continue to offer the service to the standard we had always achieved.'

Fortunately, he did persuade his Board and the RTO and so was able to use the company resources, premises and purchasing system to keep the catering service operating. He also persuaded other new companies, such as Virgin Trains, who now employed some of his previously hand-picked railway catering staff, to let them be released for Royal Train duties and so kept the best team together.

Roger Williams realised early on that the value was not in the monetary return but in the tremendous prestige associated with running the catering on such a special

MENU

Hors D'Oeuvres

Poached Sole Fillets with Grapes

Choice of Vegetables

Lemon Torte

Coffee

ROYAL TRAIN
25th June 1993

train. Indeed, Rail Gourmet was granted the Royal Warrant in 2006, which would never have been possible in British Rail days because (a) they were a nationalised industry and (b) there was no one entity responsible: this was a diverse operation where staff came from lots of different regions.

Effectively, Williams had single-handedly brought the whole catering operation under one roof from his then office at Paddington station. His current role at Rail Gourmet is in international business development, which involves travel all over the UK, Ireland and mainland Europe seeking out new business opportunities for his company. The Royal Train is really something he does in his spare time. His credentials are impressive as he has served in various capacities on the railways since 1978 when he started at the Great Eastern Hotel in Liverpool Street, London. Owned by British Rail, the Great Eastern was part of the British Transport

Menu

Wild mushrooms with broad beans
and oeuf mollet

* * *

Fillet of Welsh beef with Thyme and Madeira

* * *

Mango Crème Brûleé

Dinner,
The Royal Train

Monday,
12 July 2004

there is an unusual, coincidental, family connection as his grandfather was the Catering Manager on the Royal Train for ten years, from 1958.

Williams explained how the Royal Train catering team is recruited. 'The staff that we have on-board come from all over the country, most of them are directly employed by Rail Gourmet and two of them are employed by Virgin Trains who allow us to "borrow" them just for this work. There is no extra money involved – they all do it for the same wages they earn in their everyday work, with no bonus just because they are operating on the Royal Train.

'Buckingham Palace plans everything for the Royal Family's travel well in advance, so we receive plenty of notice when a Royal Train is required.

'I know about the programme right at the beginning of the year from EWS and I work quite closely together with Geoff Griffiths (EWS Account Manager). We'll go through the list of planned journeys and he'll say that on such and such occasion the train is going to start perhaps at Euston at midnight and we'll go to, say, Liverpool and there needs to be a breakfast served. At that point we work out the logistics of how many people are going to be on-board, because it's not just catering for the immediate Royal Family, it's also for the people who join the train to provide support for the journey and their visit arrangements for the next day, so it might be the policemen, it could be the valet, the Queen's dresser or Lady-in-Waiting or the Equerry. When I first started, over 20 years ago, there were also people like the Court Postmaster, and you were even able to post letters from the train! That no longer happens though, as over the years the number of people involved has been trimmed right back.

'Once we have the journey information confirmed, myself and Ken Moule, the Chief Steward, go through

Hotels group, which had originally been the focal point for all catering on trains across the country, as well as owning many of the grandest hotels in the UK, including Gleneagles and Turnberry. By then, though, train catering had passed to Travellers Fare and it was to this organisation that Williams transferred in 1980.

'I always remember my first trip out on a Pullman train to Manchester and experiencing "Dinner in the Diner" for the first time. It seemed to me that there was no finer way to travel.' That experience was to shape his career and life from then on.

Providing excellent service on-board trains became his *raison d'être* and so it was almost destined for him to become involved in catering on the Royal Train. In fact,

OPPOSITE: *When Prince Charles is on board in Wales, he insists on the chef using Welsh produce, as this dinner menu – complete with HRH's crest – for a dinner party held on Monday, 12 July 2004, clearly shows. (Railcare)*

LEFT: *This historic dinner service, dating back to the old London & North Western Railway Company, is sometimes used in the Dining Car in addition to the more recent, modern services they keep on board the train. (RAIL magazine)*

BELOW: *The Prince of Wales is justifiably proud of his personally embossed crockery, and a supply is kept on the Royal Train for his use alone. (RAIL magazine)*

each aspect of the journey and catering timings. If there are lunches or dinners involved we'll work out the menu content, much of which is based on Ken's own knowledge and experience of the tastes and preferences of the Principals travelling. He knows exactly the way that the Royal Family like their food, the type of meals they prefer and it is, in every sense, quite simple British fare. There is very little complexity to it, except when there's a dinner party where they have invited guests, and the majority of those take place when the Prince of Wales is on the train.

'His Royal Highness does a large amount of work connected with charities and community-based projects in different areas of the country that he's associated with, and perhaps when he is travelling to Wales or the West Country he'll have trade delegations or other key people invited to join the train. Normally it is when the train is parked at a halt somewhere. So, it might be in North Wales, for instance, or somewhere like that, and there will be a couple of hours when we serve drinks and a formal dinner. Often, where special guests are invited there is a theme to the meal so we liaise closely with the Palace, usually with HRH's Private Secretary and those who work for him in the catering side of the household, to determine the menu. Once they're happy with the choices we'll select and purchase the food and wine and take that on board and produce the meal.

'We don't have a preset budget for individual meals on the train, but we are always conscious of costs and look for the best value products we can find, sometimes this is from existing Rail Gourmet suppliers or alternately it may be from local suppliers to where the train is going, including sometimes products from the Duchy of Cornwall.

'Most of the trains travel overnight, so a member of the Royal Family may get on after they have been to a function or a dinner somewhere or perhaps to a theatre performance and then we'll take them through the night to the next place where their duties require their presence. Wherever they have joined the train, our job is to make sure they feel at home at night; that they have any refreshments they like when they board the train, that their staff are looked after and then in the morning that the appropriate trays are made up, the breakfast is laid on, and everybody's fed and ready for the day.'

Although the meals are being served in the confined space of a railway carriage, standards are never allowed to drop below those one would expect for Royalty. If The

RIGHT: *An unusual request for Geoff Griffiths, EWS Account Manager, was when he was told (at 4.25am) that one of the refrigerators had failed on the Royal Train and the milk had gone off. He asked the lady in charge of the coffee bar at Doncaster station if she could help and she was delighted to provide a supply of fresh milk. She later received a letter from the Royal Household thanking her for this assistance. It was on the same journey that The Queen's dresser also needed to borrow a hairdryer from Geoff's wife, Pam. All in a day's work! (Geoff Griffiths)*

OPPOSITE: *Coach 2919 was converted for use in the Royal Train in 1989, but has been 'mothballed' since 1998. This photograph was taken in the mid 1990s. (Railcare)*

BELOW: *After accompanying her husband Geoff to the Royal naming of No. 67029* **Royal Diamond** *at Rugeley station in October 1997, Pam Griffiths had the rare treat of taking lunch in the Household Diner. (Geoff Griffiths)*

For just such occasions the Royal dining coach has a long middle table that runs along the length of the vehicle and which can be extended to accommodate up to 12 guests. The table is laid with fine white linen cloths and dressed with beautiful arrays of flowers, gleaming silverware and sparkling glassware.

Place settings are carefully measured to ensure the appropriate space is laid for each guest. The Queen or the Prince of Wales usually sits in the centre, as host, so that they can talk to everyone and no one is left out of the conversation. As one would expect, silver service is the norm and the stewards are all fully trained to carry out their duties as if they were waiting at a State Banquet – with slightly less formality. This informality is not because of any less respect given to the dining occasion or protocol, more that the Royal Dining Carriage is quite an intimate area, where the Monarch and guests sit in relatively close proximity and where all the party is involved in dialogue with the Principal. It is this unique environment which sets the Train apart as an exceptional dining experience and one has to continually remember that the appropriate table etiquette is always more difficult when eating on the move!

Queen or the Prince of Wales is to give a reception on the Royal Train the stewards' first job will be to welcome guests on-board and offer drinks. This is generally done in one of the small private lounges as the dining area will already have been prepared for the meal service.

Always dressed immaculately, the stewards carry silver salvers with crystal glasses containing chilled champagne, Buck's Fizz or fruit juices as they mingle unobtrusively with the guests, offering and replenishing glasses. Other aperitifs such as gin and tonic, whisky and soda, red or white wine are also available and they ensure that on the Royal Train every guest feels very special!

Most receptions are likely to be in the evening. It is unusual for luncheon to be served on board the train as the Principals often leave at around 10 o'clock in the morning to start their engagements and, if they are returning by rail, it is not normally until later in the afternoon.

Whilst returning by rail is sometimes not an option for the Principals, due to the variety and number of public duties that they carry out, when they do so it is an opportunity to relax in private and afternoon tea is almost always enjoyed, as it is in every Royal residence. Even the Duke of Edinburgh, who normally drinks only coffee, likes a cup of tea in the afternoon and the Royal couple share a selection of sandwiches, cakes and warm scones, with cream and preserves.

As in most homes, breakfast is the most important meal of the day. For the Principals, it may well be the only time that day when they get to choose the food, because if they are attending a luncheon or evening engagement they will be served whatever their hosts feel is most appropriate. So, before they retire for the night on the train, they each decide what they would like for breakfast the following morning and at what time they want it served. Ken Moule is given his instructions about cereals, whether it is to be the 'Great British Breakfast' or perhaps a 'Continental' and when Martin Carter, the chef, should prepare it.

The tables are set up that night after the Principals have retired to their private quarters and then, in the morning, with the train stationed at a country halt somewhere on a quiet line, preferably with bright sunny views of a valley, riverside, wooded vale or even the coastline, breakfast is served in style. It really is the best way to travel.

Later that day, once the main party has left the train, the crew clean down and detrain themselves, normally somewhere up the line as the train is empty, working back towards Wolverton. If the train has finished in northern Scotland this could be sometime late in the evening or even the following day! Occasionally though,

they will be lucky and there will be a destination nearer to home.

The chefs and stewards on-board are all full-time railway staff, with the exception of Ken Moule who is now retired and only works the Royal Train in a part time role. The main crew were originally hand picked by Roger Williams or his predecessors and, amazingly in today's ever-changing world, two of the staff have worked on-board the Train for over 30 years, others for 20 years plus, while the 'junior' member of the regular staff has recently celebrated his 15th year of service. Even the reserve chef, who has only been with the team for a couple of years, has been on the railway for over 25 years.

There is always a nucleus of three staff on-board whatever the make up of the train set and incredibly, these three alone have over 100 years of railway service between them. The longest serving of these is Bob Bigsby, who started work in the Restaurant Car Department of British Transport Hotels back in 1967. Silver service training was standard in those days, with excellent quality menus and very experienced crews to learn from. Bob said: 'It was like being on an apprenticeship; the first thing I noticed was the skill of the waiting staff serving with speed and agility despite the movement of the train. That and the great team spirit amongst the mainly male crew, many of whom were middle-aged staff and had been working on-board since leaving school and to whom it really was a way of life.

'My first train was from London Euston up to Lake Windermere. The closest you can get to the lake by rail on the main line now is probably Oxenholme, but in those days there was a direct service. My favourite journeys on the Royal Train were during the Silver Jubilee year in 1977 and the Golden Jubilee tours in 2002, when The Queen and The Duke of Edinburgh visited many different locations around the UK and we were able to help the celebrations by catering for a number of special dinner parties during the trips.'

Post privatisation, Bob transferred to Virgin Trains and still works for them now as an on-board service manager out of London Euston on the Manchester services. Bob said: 'I've seen so many changes in trains over the years, but the one constant for me has always been the Royal Train. It is like a family on-board and it's been a great part of my life for the last 34 years.'

Both Bob Bigsby and Ken Moule were awarded the RVM by Her Majesty The Queen in recognition of their personal commitment to providing the service on the Train.

They have worked together for such a long time that the whole operation looks effortless. It's a bit like watching a swan gliding calmly across a lake with his feet working hard out of sight and of course, the Royal passengers see only the calm exterior.

'We are very careful to make sure that the atmosphere is both relaxed and politely convivial so as not to create any fuss for our special passengers,' says Roger Williams. 'But, in reality, with this crew on-board I know that I can rely on them to provide the perfect service. In fact it is a privilege to work with them and we are really like extended family to each other – it's a very close bond.'

In the days when there were more coaches used with Royal Trains there would be perhaps nine or ten catering staff employed at any one time. There were traditionally the 'two ends' to be looked after on each train, with the Royal principals at one end, but also the Household staff were catered for at the other end and there could even be a third kitchen galley depending on who was travelling.

Even though today it is a lower proportion of staff to the number of people who travel, nothing is left to chance. Although staff members have other day jobs, the Royal Train takes precedence; even their holidays are arranged around the Train's annual programme.

The design of the kitchens was based on those of mainline trains from the late 1970s. There is a range of electric cooking apparatus that is capable of preparing many more meals at one time than will ever be actually required but that again was because of the need to leave nothing to chance. Two grills, two ovens, two refrigerators and, unusually for trains, a freezer, gives Martin Carter the opportunity to practise real cuisine compared with the more modern-day fare that one may see on-board intercity trains of today.

Like Bob Bigsby, Martin started work in the Restaurant Car Department at Euston, joining straight from school in the summer of 1975. He remembers going up the main

BELOW: *The Duke of Edinburgh's kitchen is all-electric and equipped with (almost) every modern appliance. However, the chef doesn't get much opportunity to see where the Train is going as the windows are opaque. (Railcare)*

line to Carlisle working as an assistant chef on an old gas-powered kitchen car. 'They were very narrow kitchens and with two people working alongside each other you were very close to the cooking ranges. I was shocked by the heat of the gas ovens and grills and soon learnt to make sure I knew where the bumpy bits of track were. It was normal in those days to do more washing up than cooking, but that was all part of the learning curve and eventually I got the chance to work as chef in my own right. I love working on-board the Royal Train, especially when there is a dinner party. My biggest challenge was early on when we had unexpectedly been given three kitchen cars in the Train, and extra guests to cater for – I spent most of the time running between the three cars making sure all the meals were cooking properly and nothing got burnt!

'These days we have a few extra bits of equipment such as coffee makers but mainly it's how a train kitchen would have been laid out 30 years ago.'

It may come as a surprise to learn that The Queen does not bring her own chef or steward with her. The reason is quite simple. Railway staff have to be specially trained to work in a different environment; cooking on-board a moving train, carrying a tray with hot tea or coffee, pouring drinks or doing silver service travelling at 75mph is a skill that has to be acquired, and the

ABOVE: *The Royal Train's Chef, Martin Carter, is well used to working in a moving environment and, as well as cooking all meals for the Royal Family, he provides hot snacks and light meals for the Household when they are on board. (Railcare)*

Rail Gourmet team do this every day of the week. It's second nature.

Also, the chefs and stewards are well used to working in a railway environment so the logistical challenges of having to get the goods on to the train and to work in the confines of a very small area are well practised. Finally, the Royal staff who travel on-board to support the Royal party have already done a day's work, so for them it is a chance to 'refuel' and prepare for the next day's duties, wherever that may be. The Royal Household understands the limitations of the Train and the unique conditions under which the Rail Gourmet staff work, and they greatly appreciate being 'spoilt' for a change.

The Household dining car is very much like a first-class diner on an intercity train. It has a traditional coach layout with tables of four and two seats in half of the carriage and a kitchen and small store area in the other half. Other coaches in the train include smaller galleys, each one still capable of providing a full meal service.

Martin Carter splits his time between preparing hot snacks and light meals for the Household staff at one end of the train and catering for the Royal Family at the other. The Household does not get a wide choice of menus, rather Martin or Ken Moule decide what to serve and it is usually similar to whatever the Royal party is eating that day.

Ken has been Chief Steward in charge of the Royal Train service for some 28 years and worked on the railway for 37 years. He has a remarkable relationship with the members of the Royal Family and is both liked and trusted by the Principals. He explained: 'Over the

BELOW: *The Household Dining Car is similar to a first class diner on any other train, with the possible exception of the antimacassars bearing the Royal Train logo, and the pictures of former Royal Trains at either end.* *(RAIL magazine)*

years, Bob, Martin and I have found ways to make our service more efficient and cut away all the peripheral costs. We do everything from loading the stores onto the train, polishing the silverware, cooking and serving the food and even doing the washing up – there are no dishwashers on this train, only us!'

This small nucleus of a team is supported by another long-serving member, Guy Daley. While on the Royal Train he is designated as a 'steward' but he was in fact a chief steward in his own right in the 1980s and 1990s. He would take charge of the main Pullman train working from Manchester to London in the morning, serving around 120 first-class full English breakfasts, and return to Manchester in the evening with a similar fill of first-class customers, offering a four-course dinner served with fine wines. Nowadays, Guy is an on-board standards manager for Rail Gourmet, working in the UK and Ireland helping to set and monitor the service standards of the company's operations.

'Guy gives the team an extra dimension,' says Roger Williams. 'He is a very capable steward and is used to working against the clock on busy trains – he's probably worth two extra people in reality. Guy's very useful when there are special dinner parties and we have to provide and finish the service within quite tight timescales due to the Train's running times.'

Daley joined the railway in 1983 working for Travellers' Fare and soon made an impact with the restaurant car crews in Manchester. It was not long before he was promoted to Chief Steward and then to a new grade of Purser, and it was only a matter of time before he was chosen for the Royal Train.

'I really enjoy working the Train,' says Guy. 'I love the *camaraderie* amongst the crew, including all the people we meet from other parts of the railway, and the special feeling you get when you pull into a station and there are all the crowds waiting to greet The Queen or the Prince of Wales.

'Within our business, working on the Royal Train is the pinnacle of achievement and it's a great honour to be included in the team. All of us are experienced people who have worked together for many years and the boss knows he can totally rely on us. Because we're away a lot at night we have to act responsibly. The Royal Family and the Household have to know that we aren't going to say anything that would be inappropriate – or to reveal anything we might observe while serving the family or the Household staff.'

Before they are allowed anywhere near the Royal Family, the Rail Gourmet staff undergo a formal vetting and screening process that investigates every aspect of their working and personal lives. Where the Royal Train is concerned there is no appeal if an offence is committed. Once someone does something wrong, he is off the train – and there is no return ticket.

When staff were being recruited for the Royal Train it was important to pick people who would get on well together because it is quite an intimate environment. They are living together for days on end. During the Queen's Golden Jubilee year series of train journeys,

TOP RIGHT: *Seen in the Royal Dining Car are (from left) Bob Bigsby (Deputy Chief Steward), Martin Carter (Chef), Ken Moule (Chief Steward) and Roger Williams (Catering Manager).*

ABOVE: *Roger Williams in the fully-dressed and decorated Royal dining car. He always tries to find flowers suitable for the occasion.*

overnight, so in one way it was no different to that, but it did take a bit of getting used to the different layout of the train and the working routines. It's a real honour to be included.'

There are no female staff on board the Royal Train. Is this a preference that the Royal Family has shown for male servants or is it railway policy? Roger Williams says: 'It's certainly not deliberate, it's just that within the catering organisation up to twenty years ago there were very few female staff. Now probably, given that a lot of the cooks and stewards have come from airline backgrounds, like Virgin Trains for example, in association with Virgin Airlines, there is a much higher percentage of staff being female. However, I think staying away overnight and the fact that they've got to put up with fairly long hours, just traditionally has meant in the past that it's been men only. Sleeping arrangements could also be a little bit more awkward as well if you have a mixed team, but there's no reason why there shouldn't be a lady working on board the train and I wouldn't be surprised to see one in the future.'

A week before a Royal Train journey, Ken Moule, the Chief Steward, places an order with the Rail Gourmet purchasing team, who then arrange for delivery of the food and drink to their stores at Waterloo station from where they are collected by Ken and his colleagues several hours before they are due to depart. The company has 45 supply centres on stations around the country so they're delivering hundreds of thousands of products a week to go onto trains; to just about every

there were times when they were away for the best part of two weeks. One train would finish and they would be off for a day and back for another five days, so they were living together in every respect, and also the catering staff uniquely shares sleeping berths, whereas most of the other people on the train have an individual sleeping compartment.

The most recent recruit to the team is the reserve chef, Alan 'Dutch' Holland, who lives in Edinburgh. Asked how he felt when he went on-board the Royal Train for the first time he said: 'I'm used to working on charter trains where we will often have to cater for a hundred diners at a time and be away working

LEFT: *The Royal Train men seen relaxing at Llandudno station are (from left) Jim Ross (loco engineer), Nick Edwards (Royal Train Officer), Gareth Jones (Traction Inspector) and Wayne Millard (loco engineer). (Geoff Griffiths)*

train company in England, Wales and Scotland. Companies that are selected to supply Rail Gourmet have to be accredited and are generally members of the British Catering Association. They are never told in advance who the goods they are supplying are intended for. The orders are placed without any reference to Royalty, or even that they are for a 'special' customer.

Once the supplies have been checked, they are taken to Wolverton and loaded on to the Royal Train. The staff make sure that all the linen is clean, the silverware is polished and the crockery is free from any damage and everything is in pristine condition. If there's a dinner party, tables will be laid up, the flowers are collected from the florist, and final checks made to see that the right food has been delivered and prepared ready for those boarding in the evening. If it is to be an evening departure at 11 o'clock, the catering staff will eat their own evening meals at 7pm to give them plenty of time to prepare. Once the Royal party has joined the Train, the stewards serve the meals or light refreshments. Only after that work has been completed can the stewards prepare for the morning, when they serve the breakfasts and prepare the 'calling trays' of tea or coffee (Earl Grey for Her Majesty, with no sugar, and coffee for Prince Philip). The stewards do not carry the trays into the Royal bedrooms; the Travelling Footman takes the Duke

of Edinburgh's and Her Majesty's dresser does it for The Queen, as male servants are not allowed to enter a lady's bedroom while she is still there. Ken Moule says there were exceptions in the past for other members of the Family.

Once the principals have departed from the train it returns to its Wolverton 'home' and the staff disperse to their various home towns. They are certainly spread far and wide across the country and with locations such as Eastbourne, Wolverhampton, Trowbridge, Manchester, Southend and Edinburgh, they have a geographical coverage that means they often don't see each other again until the next Royal Train.

The relationship between the Royal Family and the men who look after them on the Train is unique, perhaps even more so than that enjoyed by all but a few at the Royal residences. With such longevity of service running throughout the core team, the stewards have served several different generations including the Royal children. Palace etiquette does not apply as formally on the train as it does at Windsor or Buckingham Palace, but this does not imply that there is any less respect.

The staff are obviously very polite, but they are quite 'bubbly' when the Royal Family is around. From the crew's point of view and also from the Principals' side, there is a real sense of affinity and appreciation for the service provided and the care taken to always make sure that the Train feels like a travelling 'home'. This is somewhere that can be a haven from the formality of the public engagements they are preparing for or returning from.

Members of the Royal Family know the staff by their Christian names; conversations are held about holidays, families and hobbies and in the past, various gestures of goodwill have been given by the Family to the staff, including permission to join the Household Staff's Christmas celebrations and sporting events.

Ken Moule and Bob Bigsby are especially well known characters and there is a genuine interest shown in their welfare. On one occasion, Ken had badly injured his shoulder in a fall and was off work for several weeks. When the Prince of Wales heard of this he recommended an expert consultant surgeon to him – a course of action which ended with Ken fully recovered and back to work, fighting fit. It's that type of relationship.

During one of the busiest periods on board the train, the 2002 Golden Jubilee Tour of the United Kingdom, the

staff had worked the Train to Cardiff for what they assumed would be a one-way trip. However, due to a problem with the aircraft that was scheduled to bring The Queen and the Duke of Edinburgh back to London, it was decided that they would return by rail. Ken Moule was washing up in the galley when Prince Philip came in unexpectedly and enquired what they would be having for dinner. Ken told him the cupboard was bare, as they had only stocked up for one leg of the journey, but to leave it to him. So, as The Queen and the Prince carried out their engagements in Cardiff and with no time to get to Bristol where the nearest main Rail Gourmet service centre was, Ken went down the local shops and managed to get enough provisions to supply them with a three-course dinner.

It was during the same period that the staff were suddenly asked if they could mount a dinner for six people in the Duke of Edinburgh's private dining coach. Normally, the table in there will seat only four, but by removing some of the furniture, including the sofa,

armchair and sideboard, they would be able to cope. While they were doing this His Royal Highness strolled into the carriage, where he usually liked to sit and enjoy a drink and read his newspaper. When he saw they hadn't finished with the removal, without asking he picked up one end of the sofa and helped Ken carry it out of the coach. Not quite the image of the Duke of Edinburgh the public normally sees.

Sometimes there is a slight mischievousness about the Train staff which causes a lighter moment or two, particularly where it involves a member of the Royal Household. In late 2007, Sir (now Lord) Robin Janvrin, retired as Private Secretary to The Queen. On his last journey on the Royal Train, Ken Moule and his colleagues, who had a marvellous working relationship with him, decided to mark his retirement by hiring and wearing full dress white tropical Royal Navy uniforms (Lord Janvrin is a former naval officer), and 'piping' him on board. The leg pull was appreciated fully by the Principals as Ken and Bob continued to wear the uniforms as they served dinner!

In another demonstration of the relationship not only with the Principals but with the Household staff as well, the Rail Gourmet staff have, on occasions, been invited to play the Household team at golf in the grounds of both Windsor Castle and on the Balmoral Estate. With the grand backdrop of the castle at Windsor or the scenic beauty of the hills and Royal Deeside valley at Balmoral, the Train staff have enjoyed several games, although they have not always been on the winning side!

'Sometimes we have been greeted by members of the Royal Family as they have walked or driven through the grounds,' said Ken, 'but my golf isn't good enough for it to be a spectator sport yet!'

LEFT: *In the mid 1950s, three new saloons were built for the use of Prince Charles, Princess Anne, and senior royal courtiers, together with a new principal Royal Dining Car. (Railcare)*

RIGHT: *In the years immediately after the Second World War, most of the Royal Train coaches dated back to the 1930s and before. But here, the table is being laid c1947 in the ex-LNWR twelve-wheel dining saloon No. 76, built in 1900. This remained in use until 1956. (Patrick Kingston Collection)*

There is no doubt that the Monarch accepts them in a unique and personal way. Every person who has worked on the Royal Train has been invited to a Royal Household function. Together with their wives, they have all been to either a Garden Party at Buckingham Palace or to the most exclusive of all Palace staff outings, the annual Christmas Ball. A full evening dress event, it gives the Royal Family an opportunity to thank the staff who have been so loyal throughout the year. It is also a thank you to the partners of the staff who have put up with their other half being away so much and, because of the staff's familiar faces, members of the Royal Family will invariably stop and chat when they recognise a member of the Train team in the crowd.

In addition to these events, one of the memorable moments for Ken Moule was being invited to attend the Royal Wedding of The Prince of Wales and Lady Diana Spencer in 1981 in St Paul's Cathedral. Similarly, for Roger Williams, attending the service to celebrate the Diamond Wedding Anniversary of The Queen and Prince Philip in Westminster Abbey in 2007 was very special. 'Such occasions are extraordinary parts of the history of our nation,' said Roger, 'and are remembered for the rest of your life. Places you visit on the train can also be memorable too. For example, when The Queen travelled on the Train to the launching of the P&O liner *Oriana* at Southampton, it was amazing just to see the size of the ship dwarfing the Train as we pulled alongside it on the side of the docks. When the Prince of Wales drove the steam engine across the Ribblehead Viaduct on the Settle to Carlisle line the view from the Train down into the valley was really superb. I feel really privileged to have had the chance to make those journeys.'

Up until the mid-1990s, there were many occasions when the Royal Train was used to transport incoming Heads of State arriving in the United Kingdom for a State Visit. If they were landing at Gatwick Airport, a member of the Royal Family would travel with the Train to meet the very important guest and return with them to London's Victoria station where the Head of State would be greeted and welcomed by The Queen.

A special waiting room at Victoria would be set aside for the welcoming ceremony. Rail Gourmet would dress this with flowers and arrange refreshments for Her Majesty while she waited for the train to arrive. That incoming Head of State's first impression of Britain was travelling on the Royal Train and so the service had to be absolutely impeccable.

It was up to the Train's catering staff to make sure that the VIP visitor was comfortable, fed and refreshed ready for his Royal introduction. 'It was probably the most stressful of the various types of Royal Train journey,' said Williams. 'There was very limited time and we were often asked to provide very specific sorts of food which was sometimes both difficult to source and had to be prepared in a special way. Getting this wrong could have meant deeply offending a visiting Head of State only a few minutes prior to them meeting The Queen, which was not a responsibility to be taken lightly.'

The catering staff may be among the most trusted of Royal servants, but they never confuse friendliness with familiarity. They all know that when they are serving The Queen, however friendly she might be towards them, she is still the Monarch, and they never forget it for a moment. They are also devoted to Her Majesty and her family and whatever they request the chefs and stewards will deliver.

If liver and bacon is wanted for breakfast or if they just feel like Kellogg's Cornflakes, that's what is served, and if they want refreshments in the early hours of the morning that's not a problem. There is very little grandeur once the doors are closed and the train is on the move. It is a very trusting relationship – on both sides – and that's why it works so well.

THE CATERING STAFF also have, on occasion, to look after The Queen and other members of the Royal Family when they are travelling on scheduled rail services other than on the Royal Train. Roger Williams remembers well the call from Eurostar, to ask him to organise the Royal Party's catering when Her Majesty travelled as a guest on the inaugural run of the Eurostar train through the Channel Tunnel in 1994. 'The Operations Director of Eurostar phoned me asking for help as he had brand-new catering contractors who had never served on-board before. It was such an important day with The Queen and the Prime Minister travelling through to Calais to join in a ceremony with President Mitterand that it was more appropriate for our staff to manage the service.'

It was not such a popular decision with the Eurostar staff and really caused a rumpus with the contractors, but to Williams, Moule and Bigsby it was just another journey with their special customer.

On another occasion when The Queen visited Portsmouth, a normal South West Trains service was used. Two of the Royal Train stewards travelled with her and, using an ordinary catering trolley parked up in a first-class compartment, prepared and served afternoon tea, including freshly made sandwiches and cakes, in the reserved area at the back of the train. They brought the chinaware from the Royal Train and the journey passed swiftly and enjoyably. On the way back, however, things were not so well organised for a change. In an unusual turn of events, having gone for a walk in Portsmouth while The Queen carried out her official function, the stewards took a wrong turn and got lost. Trying to retrace their steps made the situation worse and they found themselves further away than ever from Harbour station. With only minutes remaining before the train was due to depart there was only one thing left to do – run! They just made it back and actually joined the train after The Queen. However, in their customary manner the service was delivered impeccably and no-one was any the wiser.

CHAPTER 3

The train today

T IS ONLY on very rare occasions that all nine coaches of the Royal Train are utilised into a single train, and then only when all four principals, The Queen, the Duke of Edinburgh, the Prince of Wales and the Duchess of Cornwall, are travelling together.

An example of this happening was on 8 November 2007 when they all joined the train to travel from London to Cardiff where Her Majesty was to formally open the Welsh Assembly. On this occasion, The Queen and Prince Philip got on in Paddington with Prince Charles and the Duchess meeting them at Patchway near Bristol, having been driven from their home at Highgrove in Gloucestershire. Otherwise, the usual configuration is a seven-coach train, or eight if the Duchess of Cornwall travels with her husband.

As the man responsible for maintaining and servicing the Royal coaches, Chris Hillyard has been looking after them for over twenty-five years from his base at

LEFT: *There can be few sights more evocative of the Golden Age of Steam than this view of the Royal Train on the Settle & Carlisle line on 22 March 2005. This is the empty train heading north from Wolverton to Aberdeen behind ex-LMS No. 6233* **Duchess of Sutherland** *to collect the Prince of Wales and then convey him to Liverpool. (Geoff Griffiths).*

Wolverton near Milton Keynes in Buckinghamshire.

Chris travels on every Royal Train journey (he has been described as 'the glue' that holds the whole thing together) and has 31 years of service on the Royal Train, having undertaken 769 journeys travelling some 471,678 miles to date. He acts, with Geoff Griffiths of EWS, as the interface between the Royal Household and the railway companies, including Network Rail, who operate the rail infrastructure, English Welsh & Scottish Railway (EWS), the Royal Train operators, Rail Gourmet, who provide all the meals and drinks on board, British Transport Police, the Fire Service, and any other organisation that might be involved in the hundreds of details that have to be worked out before every Royal journey.

It is Chris who 'meets and greets' the Royal

passengers and because he has been doing the job for so many years, his face has naturally become familiar to every member of the Royal Family. They see him when they arrive at the departing station and he is there to bid them goodbye when they leave the train. In 2002, Her Majesty recognised his contribution to the smooth running of the Royal Train by awarding him the Royal Victorian Medal, her personal Order of Chivalry, which is given by her without 'advice' from Downing Street, or anyone else.

The responsibility for the furnishings of the saloons, the bed linen, the carpets, curtains and laundry, lies with Chris Hillyard and his small team at Wolverton. He says things do not get changed all that frequently as they are constrained by budget, but as the train is obviously not used on a daily basis, it does not suffer the wear and tear that a normal overnight sleeper or dining car would. The moment the train arrives back at the depot from a journey, the team descend on it to see what needs repairing, washing or cleaning. Two part-time ladies look after the domestic side of the Royal Train, vacuuming and dusting, and they take a particular pride in the fact that not a speck of dust is found once they have been through the saloons.

After completing their Royal journeys, they are thoroughly cleaned inside and out, with fresh linen placed in all the saloons; the bathrooms and showers have new soap, toilet requisites and towels supplied; the curtains and carpets are examined for tears and stains; any minor repairs (they rarely have major problems) are attended to, and within hours of the coaches being back in their home base, they are ready to be pulled out onto the track 'dressed' ready for the next journey, even if it is some weeks away. Nothing is left to chance and a large supply of spare parts is kept in the immaculate stores as well as emergency supplies, which are carried on board.

Two support vehicles are attached to the Royal Train when it is travelling: one at either end. The first doubles as staff living quarters with dining facilities, showers and small bedroom cabins, similar to those found on overnight express trains. They even have their own travelling telephone exchange. This coach also carries a supply of extra toiletries, blankets and pillows and spare parts in case of equipment breakdown or if the journey takes longer than planned, although this is such an unusual occurrence that no-one currently employed at Wolverton can recall when it last happened.

The other support coach is the power car. It is fitted with a Rolls-Royce diesel generator which allows the train to be kept supplied with all necessary services, such as air conditioning, water, heating and sanitation, and also keeps all the systems alive and working freely. This means the power unit can do everything that's required to provide The Queen and her family with (almost) all the comforts of home.

BELOW: *The current 'power' car, No. 2920, undergoing testing at Derby. This vehicle is fitted with a Rolls-Royce 350kW diesel generator to provide the Royal Train with all essential services. It includes Household staff sleeping accommodation. (Railcare)*

On the train, the technical staff provide service back-up to the on-train electrical and mechanical systems in compliance with working time directives and Safety Critical Working Regulations (ROGS 2006).

Railcare staff are required to assist Royal Household personnel when they are loading and unloading luggage and cooperating with RPG staff regarding the security systems on the train. They are also needed when the coaches are hooked up to the locomotives and when the train is shunted into its assembled form at Wolverton. The staff are trained in basic first-aid and resuscitation techniques and they would act as fire and evacuation wardens in the event of emergency.

The advent of mobile telephones has made life much more comfortable for everyone on board and the men who work alongside. In the early days of the Royal Train, it used to be the task of some poor unfortunate engineer from British Telecom (or GPO as it then was) to shy up the nearest telephone pole in all winds and weathers when the train was stopped at night, and then drag a cable across a field or two in order to connect it to the mains. That was the sort of rudimentary 'Heath Robinson' contraption that passed for communications in those days. Now, of course, the only problem they have is that there are still some 'black-spot' areas in the country where mobile phones cannot receive a signal. The train operators have contingency procedures for such occurrences as they do for fire evacuation or any form of attack.

When The Queen is planning her engagements for the coming year, she and Prince Philip indicate when and where they would prefer to use the Royal Train. Her Majesty's Private Secretary will then forward the information to the Director of Royal Travel, Group Captain Timothy Hewlett, a former Royal Air Force fighter pilot, who not only handles all the requirements for the Royal Train, but also every flight that members of the Royal Family take, from single helicopter trips and journeys by fixed-wing aircraft of No 32 (The Royal) Squadron based at Northolt, to leasing Boeing 747s for long-haul overseas tours.

The travel office is located on the ground floor at Buckingham Palace and the total staff including Tim Hewlett is just three: two male and one female. Between them they organise all the travel requirements of every member of the Royal Family.

Tim Hewlett explained how the system works with regard to the Royal Train. 'The first indication we get is when we have sight of, in The Queen and the Duke of Edinburgh's case, their semi-annual diary, so towards the end of the year we get to see the proposed diary for The Queen up until June/July the following year. We then scan that carefully and look to see if there's an away day in Cornwall, Scotland or Wales and it will often have 'Train?' on the diary, so if there's a hint of anything that we see as being a potential train journey we will log it on our database in the Travel Office on the Royal Travel Diary. We will almost immediately go to our contacts at EWS who currently manage the train and give them advanced warning of a Royal Train movement to Cornwall, Devon, Glasgow, Wales, or wherever it happens to be, so at least they have it in their diary.

'The details, such as exactly which station Her Majesty wants to stop at or embark or disembark, exactly what time she would like to be at the destination and whether she is coming back by train or flying back by fixed-wing plane or helicopter, emerges in the months preceding the engagement. There is a vast amount of telephoning and e-mailing between the various organisations involved in a Royal Train journey with a great deal of checking and cross-checking. But the people who operate the train have many years', experience, which ensures that things

ABOVE: When The Queen and the Duke of Edinburgh arrived at Scunthorpe, Lincolnshire on 31 July 2002 they were presented with – what else? – a gift of Lincolnshire sausages! (Mick Foster)

*OPPOSITE: Hauled by No. 6233 **Duchess of Sutherland**, the Royal Train arrives at Holyhead, on Anglesey, during the Golden Jubilee tours of the United Kingdom in 2002. This magnificent steam locomotive attracted huge attention wherever it appeared. (John F. Stiles)*

go smoothly. They are able to anticipate any potential problems and so avoid them. And we all know that The Queen has given express orders that the Royal Train must not inconvenience other rail users.

'Some years are busier than others. For example, the Jubilee Tour of 2002 was very active. Greater use was made of the train and it was supplemented with an additional carriage that was converted to an office, because there were at least two events when The Queen was away on the train for up to three days at a time. Her Majesty used the train going around Wales and again in Scotland, where she accessed some of the more remote parts of the country and she stayed on board for two or three nights. So an extra coach was needed to provide the private secretaries with a limited form of office facility and more people than usual travelled with The Queen.'

Geoff Griffiths is the initial point of contact between the railway industry and the Royal Household. The first indication he receives that a train is required will be a telephone call from Tim Hewlett at Buckingham Palace or occasionally from Clarence House, but it does not always follow that both parties can be satisfied at once, as there is no longer any facility for operating two trains on the same day. If, for example, the Prince of Wales's office ask for a train on a particular day and The Queen's private secretary has previously made the same request, then obviously Her Majesty's requirements receive prior attention. It does not often happen, as Royal engagements are planned many months in advance, but there have been odd occasions when Prince Charles has been forced to give way to his mother.

When the Prince was first married to the late Diana, Princess of Wales, they made considerable use of the Royal Train, either together or separately. It was only after the birth of her children that the Princess decided not to use the train as often on the grounds that she preferred not to stay away overnight, but to return to London – or Highgrove – in time to put them to bed. A glance at the timetable of the Royal Train between July 1981 and May 1982 shows how much use of it the couple made.

RIGHT: *Because the Golden Jubilee tours involved so many three-day journeys, an extra coach, No. 2918, was attached for use as an office by the Royal Household. This was the Private Secretary's and Equerry's room, equipped with a direct telephone link to and from The Queen. (Railcare)*

1981–82	MEMBER OF THE ROYAL FAMILY	JOURNEY DETAILS	RAILWAY	STOCK
29 July 1981	TRH The Prince and Princess of Wales	London Waterloo–Romsey Locomotive No 73142 (Honeymoon special)	BR	MkII 1st, MkI brake composite, general manager's saloon
26–30 October 1981	TRH The Prince and Princess of Wales	London Euston–Shotton Bangor–Fishguard Harbour Haverfordwest–Carmarthen Swansea–Builth Road Cardiff–London Paddington (1,247 miles) Nos 87028 *Lord President* 47449 *Fair Rosamund* 47511 *Thames*	BR	2906, 2901, 2900, 2902, 2013, 45000, 325, 2905, SLS2500
11/12 November 1981	TRH The Prince and Princess of Wales	London King's Cross–York (460 miles) No 47577 *Benjamin Gimbert GC* (TRH's visit to the National Railway Museum)	BR	2906, 2013, 2901, 2902, 45000, 2900, 2905, 2909
29/30 March 1982	TRH The Prince and Princess of Wales	Aberdeen–Leeds Leeds–London King's Cross (1,120 miles) Nos 87005 *City of London* 47461 *Charles Rennie Mackintosh*	BR	2906, 2908, 2901, 2902, 2911, 2900, 2905, 2909
1/2 April 1982	TRH The Prince and Princess of Wales	London Euston–Liverpool (425 miles) Nos 87004 *Britannia* 47439 and 47501	BR	2906, 2908, 2901, 2902, 2911, 2900, 2905, 2909
26/27 April 1982	TRH The Prince and Princess of Wales	Bodmin Road–London Paddington (620 miles) No 47511 *Thames*	BR	2906, 2908, 2901, 2902, 2911, 2900, 2905, 2909
29/30 April 1982	HRH The Prince of Wales	London Paddington–Carmarthen (570 miles) Nos 47511 *Thames* 31423	BR	2906, 2901, 2911, 2908, 2905
13/14 May 1982	TRH The Prince and Princess of Wales	Aberdeen–Milton Keynes Milton Keynes–London Euston (1,050 miles) Nos 86211 *City of Milton Keynes* 47427 (The Prince detrained at Milton Keynes)	BR	2906, 2908, 2901, 2902, 2911, 2900, 2905, 2909

ABOVE: *EWS Class 66 locomotive No. 66187 draws the Royal carriages from an overnight stabling point during the Prince of Wales's journey from Aberdeen to Abergavenny in January 2002. (Mick Foster)*

Because the train is configured with sleeping accommodation, many people believe it travels only throughout the night; it doesn't.

An important ingredient for all overnight stops is to arrange the stabling facilities which are the secluded sidings, close to the final destination where the train remains throughout the night. The fact that even today these places are referred to as 'stables' with the tracks called 'roads' and the railway coaches called 'carriages' is a throwback to the time when travel was by horse-drawn carriage.

The Royal passengers are able to have a good night's sleep while the train is stationary, parked within an hour or so of their final stop. This means they are then able to rise, bathe, dress, have a leisurely breakfast and then be briefed by their private secretary on the day's programme as the train completes its journey into the station, making sure they do not disrupt any normal rail schedules. One of the overriding principles of Royal travel – and that includes trains and planes – is that it should be carried out with the minimum disruption to the public. So, if there happens to be a scheduled service with a ten o'clock arrival or departure from the platform also allocated to the Royal Train, the operators

will have made sure it is due to arrive at, say, 09.50 or 10.10, and Royal attention to detail being what it is, the doors open at exactly the right moment – and at the right place.

It is often wondered how it is that whenever The Queen arrives at a railway station, her doors always open at the right spot on the platform – where the red carpet has been laid (on the rare occasions when there is one) and where the local dignitaries are all lined up. The answer is deceptively simple and not in the least high-tech: Network Rail will have measured the distance between the driver's cab on the locomotive and The Queen's double doors. They then place a man with a yellow flag on the exact spot where the driver has to stop. When the driver sees his colleague with the flag he knows just where he should be – and it usually works! Human nature being what it is, however, inevitably there have been occasions when the man with the flag has automatically stepped back a pace or two as the massive engine approaches, much to the dismay of the greeting party when they see their Royal guest drifting past the appointed place. It doesn't happen very often, but when it does, the Train Officer and Train Foreman want to know the reason; excuses are not tolerated.

ABOVE LEFT: *Nothing is left to chance. The platform is measured prior to the arrival of the Royal Train to establish exactly where each coach will halt.* (Geoff Griffiths)

ABOVE: *Then a railway employee, bearing a yellow flag, is positioned at the precise spot where the engine needs to stop so that Her Majesty is able to step from her coach at exactly the right point on the platform. It is a system, as seen here at Newcastle, that has barely changed since Queen Victoria's day.* (Geoff Griffiths)

LEFT: *And it all works! The Lord Lieutenant of Northumberland greets his Sovereign at Berwick-on-Tweed in July 2001 as Chris Hillyard guards the door of The Queen's coach.* (Mick Foster)

Occasionally, the Royal Train is scheduled to stop at a small halt in the countryside with only enough space on its single platform for perhaps one and a half coaches. When that happens, the Royal passenger still alights where he or she is supposed to, of course, with the rest of party having to walk the length of the train in order to get off.

Once the household has made the request, Geoff Griffiths draws up a plan of the train, which can vary, depending on which member of the Royal Family is travelling. As the majority of journeys these days involve an overnight stop, the first people to be contacted are Network Rail, who are told where the train needs to go and the route they wish to follow.

After agreeing the route, the number and suitability of engines to be used is determined as some are too heavy

ABOVE: *The Royal Train
arrives at Rugeley station,
Staffordshire, on 12 October
2007 prior to the naming
ceremony of locomotive
No. 67029* **Royal Diamond**
by The Queen.
(Geoff Griffiths)

for certain lines. From EWS's large fleet of diesel
locomotives, two are designated as power units to the
Royal Train. These are Class 67 Nos 67005 *Queen's
Messenger* and 67006 *Royal Sovereign*, both of which
were named by The Queen. Built at a cost of £1.5 million
each in 1999, the locomotives are identical and are based
at EWS's Toton depot in Nottinghamshire and are
painted in traditional Royal Claret and carry a 'By
Appointment' badge on the side. They are capable of
speeds up to 125mph, but like all 30 of the type are
currently only authorised to 110mph but when on Royal
duty are further restricted to 100mph. These two
celebrity locomotives now run on 100 per cent biofuel
and are expected to last at least thirty years.

While these Nos 67005 and 67006 power most of
the Royal journey's they are not retained exclusively
for Royal Train duties and they are often seen pulling
the Venice Simplon-Orient-Express in the UK, and
other luxury trains. There is also a third locomotive
kept as a reserve, No 67029 *Royal Diamond*, named
by Her Majesty in celebration of her Diamond
Wedding Anniversary in 2007 and is in silver livery.

Next, the drivers are selected. These come from a
pool of elite, vastly experienced engine drivers, all
with many years' service on the railways. The choice
of driver depends on his familiarity with the road
he is taking the train. Also, under present regulations,
drivers are only permitted to work for a little

over three hours without a break.

The station that is the final destination has to be inspected to see if there are any unforeseen obstacles that might create difficulties in moving from the train to the car that will be waiting. If The Queen is the 'client' (which is how the railways refer to their Royal passengers), the platform she will use to alight from the train is inspected and it is checked to see if there is a bridge she has to climb to reach her car, or if there is an underpass; if so, how long will it take her to walk, and will her security officers allow it anyway? British Transport Police are involved in this aspect of the planning.

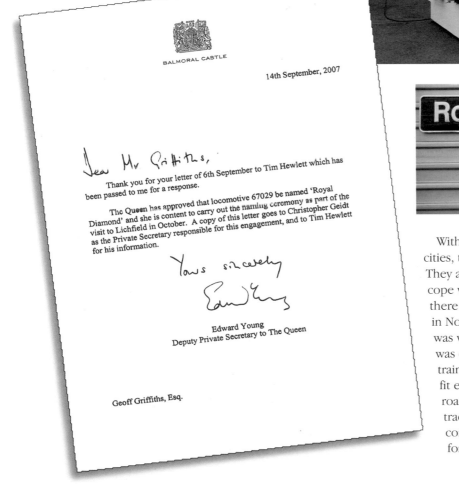

BALMORAL CASTLE

14th September, 2007

Dear Mr Griffiths,

Thank you for your letter of 6th September to Tim Hewlett which has been passed to me for a response.

The Queen has approved that locomotive 67029 be named 'Royal Diamond' and she is content to carry out the naming ceremony as part of the visit to Lichfield in October. A copy of this letter goes to Christopher Geidt as the Private Secretary responsible for this engagement, and to Tim Hewlett for his information.

Yours sincerely

Edward Young

Edward Young
Deputy Private Secretary to The Queen

Geoff Griffiths, Esq.

ABOVE: *Her Majesty is applauded as she unveils the* **Royal Diamond** *nameplate, in an historic ceremony to mark the Diamond Wedding Anniversary of The Queen and the Duke of Edinburgh, who were married in Westminster Abbey in 1947. The letter to Geoff Griffiths from Her Majesty's Deputy Private Secretary confirms her approval of the name* **Royal Diamond** *and her agreement to carry out the ceremony.*
(Geoff Griffiths)

With certain stations in large towns and cities, there are not too many problems. They already have long platforms that can cope with a nine-carriage train. However, there was an unusual incident at Tal-y-Cafn in North Wales when the Prince of Wales was visiting this part of his Principality, it was discovered that his section of the train (with the double doors) could not fit easily into the platform as there is a road running directly adjacent to the track with a level crossing. So the local constabulary simply closed the crossing for the time it took for the Prince to leave the train – with his coach on the platform and the rest of the train stranded across a busy road. It made a marvellous picture for the local photographers.

Everything is timed down to the last second and once the timings have been finalised the plan is submitted to Buckingham Palace (or Clarence House) for approval. Inevitably there will be further queries and then the Household and representatives of the railway organisations carry out a recce visit, stop-watch in hand, checking and checking again every inch of the proposed journey. Once all the arrangements have been finalised, they are sent to The Queen for her approval, as nothing is 'set in stone' until it has received Royal consent.

When you compare the running of the Royal Train today with that of the early decades of The Queen's

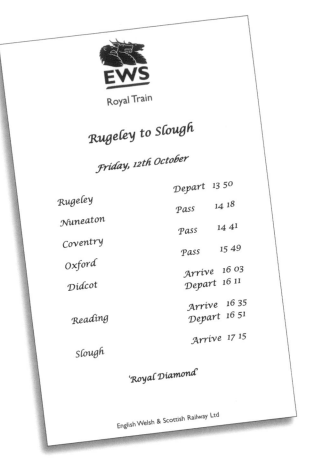

EWS
Royal Train

Rugeley to Slough

Friday, 12th October

Rugeley	Depart	13 50
Nuneaton	Pass	14 18
Coventry	Pass	14 41
Oxford	Pass	15 49
Didcot	Arrive	16 03
	Depart	16 11
Reading	Arrive	16 35
	Depart	16 51
Slough	Arrive	17 15

'Royal Diamond'

English Welsh & Scottish Railway Ltd

BELOW: *An earlier locomotive naming ceremony, at Euston station, London, on 6 December 2000. The significance of this occasion was that No. 67005* **Queen's Messenger** *was the first Alstom-built Class 67 1,860kW Bo-Bo diesel-electric to haul the Royal Train. (EWS)*

reign, one can see that life for the railway authorities has, at least in some respects, become far easier. In the 1950s and early '60s, the Western Region of British Railways had several Royal coaches that they kept strictly for their own use in that region. Similarly, the Eastern Region also had two or three ex-Edwardian coaches that were housed at Bounds Green in London to be used for the journeys to the now-closed Wolferton station via King's Lynn for the Sandringham Estate in Norfolk. In fact, every region maintained its own Royal coaches and there were far more Royal Trains seen throughout the country than there are today. In the latter stages of the 1960s it was decided to concentrate the Royal Train at Wolverton under one roof and with the advent of motorways and the increasing use of helicopters for short flights, the need for a number of these Royal carriages was reduced.

All the Royal lounge areas are full-width spanning the entire breadth of the coach. There are no corridors, so staff and household do not go through unless they have very good reasons to do so. They know the Royal Family want to be left alone when they are on board and everything that needs attention is done before the passengers join the train.

The Queen's saloon No 2903

Her Majesty's personal saloon is now over thirty years old, having been brought into service, along with the Duke's saloon (No 2904), in 1977 when both were used extensively during the Silver Jubilee tours. They were built as prototype Mark 3 passenger vehicles, which were then converted to their present status in 1976/1977. The predecessors to these two coaches were built at Wolverton in 1942, during severe wartime restrictions, and new Royal carriages were considered to be a matter of some urgency at that time to replace the wooden bodied Edwardian Royal saloons built in 1902.

At first glance the Mark 3 looks similar to its forerunners, but there is an external difference discernible to the experienced railway eye in that they have a ridged roof compared to the smooth roof of the Mark 2.

The bodyshell of the Queen's saloon is 75ft long with an important advantage over the Mark 2 as it is fitted with secondary air suspension giving the passengers, Royal and otherwise, an exceptionally smooth and comfortable ride.

Her Majesty's saloon has a bedroom, decorated in light pastel shades, with a 3ft-wide single bed in one corner (there are no double beds on the Royal Train), and the bed clothes are made up of cotton sheets and woollen blankets. The Queen's pillows are trimmed with lace, with a small Royal cipher in one corner (Prince Philip's are plain). Subdued strip lighting in the ceiling provides the main illumination but there are also several small reading lamps strategically placed to enable The Queen to read in bed if she so wishes.

The adjoining bathroom has a full-size bath (but nowhere near as large as the one Her Majesty has at Buckingham Palace). The fittings in the bathroom are modest and functional, in keeping with The Queen's desire to keep things as simple as possible and her bathroom could be replicated fairly inexpensively by anyone going into any decent showroom. The towels are white, soft and fluffy and the train operators make sure that the train is not crossing any bumpy points that would cause the water to slop over the top of the

bath, at around 7.30 in the morning, which is when The Queen is taking her bath.

The sitting room is equipped with a sofa with hand-stitched velvet cushions, and armchairs and a small dining table where she and Prince Philip always enjoy breakfast together. The table can be extended to seat six people and occasionally The Queen will invite senior members of the Royal Household who are travelling with her, to join her for dinner. There is also a desk and chair in one corner where Her Majesty works on her 'boxes' of official papers that follow her wherever she is, anywhere in the world. Even on board the Royal Train, after a full day's engagements, she cannot relax until she has spent an hour or two reading

ABOVE: *This former LMS lamp, presented to The Queen on 11 June 2002, is mounted on the wall of her saloon, near the double doors. (RAIL magazine)*

ABOVE: *The Royal Train is seen in April 2008 near Tal-y-Cafn, in North Wales, where the shorter than usual platform made it slightly difficult to cope with the length of the seven-coach train being used by the Prince of Wales. But, as usual, they managed to solve the problem in time for His Royal Highness to leave the train – at precisely the right spot.*
(Geoff Griffiths)

and initialling the papers her private secretary has prepared for her.

The vestibule at the end of The Queen's saloon contains the double doors on either side that open onto the platform once the train has arrived at its destination.

Also in the saloon, alongside The Queen's bedroom, is a room for her personal assistant and senior dresser, Angela Kelly, the woman who is arguably closer to Her Majesty than almost any other member of the Household and is regarded as being among the most influential of The Queen's servants. Miss Kelly has a bedroom and en suite shower, plus large wardrobes for The Queen's outfits.

The walls of The Queen's apartments are adorned with paintings of Scottish landscapes by the artist Roy Penny and there are also prints of earlier Royal Train journeys. The overall impression one gets is that the saloon is restful and very quiet, owing to the thick carpets that cover the floors from end to end. Privacy is maintained by the curtains that hang from every window and which can be fully drawn when required, with net drapes that enable The Queen to look out but prevent anyone looking in.

The Duke of Edinburgh's saloon No 2904

Prince Philip uses the train as a mobile office when he is on board; he hates the thought of wasting any moment in the day. So, his saloon is not regarded simply as somewhere for him to relax and do nothing. Like his daughter, the Princess Royal, (who is no longer allowed to use the Royal Train), Prince Philip believes a day doing nothing is a day wasted. His saloon is more masculine in appearance as you would expect. There is also one extra piece of equipment that The Queen's does not possess: an all-electric kitchen, which can provide meals for up to a dozen people.

As Prince Philip often uses the train on his own, this means the carriage can be attached without having to take the entire Royal Train. His Royal Highness's sitting room contains the usual sofa, armchairs and desk and also a table that can be extended to accommodate twelve people for luncheon or dinner, or used, as it more usually is, as a conference table. The armchairs in Prince Philip's sitting room are comfortable but not of the deep 'sink down' and relax type so often found in Gentlemen's clubs or country houses as the Prince does

LEFT: *A prized souvenir in the Duke of Edinburgh's saloon is this small section of railway line from Brunel's broad gauge, presented to him in 1985 to mark the 150th anniversary of the Great Western Railway. (Peter Nicholson)*

not encourage visitors to overstay their welcome. He treats the saloon as his office and nearly all the people he invites to join him are there on official business, not for purely social reasons.

The bedroom is a duplicate of The Queen's single bed, dressing table and reading lamps, but the bathroom does not contain a bath. Prince Philip will not spend the time relaxing in a bath; he prefers a shower, even at home, and his tiny bathroom also has a unique invention of his own. His magnified shaving mirror is placed at face level to the right of the lavatory so that he can sit and shave at the same time. Who knows, perhaps other busy men in their own homes could adopt his timesaving innovation?

A small section of rail, which is a souvenir of Brunel's original broad gauge, was presented to the Duke on the 150th anniversary of the founding of the Great Western Railway, and is preserved in a place of honour in his saloon, along with a more recent presentation: a blown-up version of his Senior Railcard which was given to him when he became eligible on 10 June 1987. No-one knows if he has yet taken advantage of its discount privileges. The Duke of Gloucester, arguably the Royal Family's most enthusiastic rail traveller, also has a Senior Railcard that he uses whenever he travels on a 'non-Royal' passenger train.

The Prince of Wales's saloons; dining car No 2916 and sleeping car No 2922

There are two coaches used by the Prince of Wales and the Duchess of Cornwall. They were built, originally for him, between 1983 and 1985, when the Prince and the late Diana, Princess of Wales, used them. The Duchess now uses the Princess's former sleeping car. Prince Charles was involved a great deal in the early layout of the saloons and he ordered a number of features that are not standard, even in the Royal Train. He personally chose the pictures for his sleeping car comprising eleven

paintings and drawings, which combine to make the coach appear more like home perhaps, although a little cramped. The painting immediately over his bed is of the former Royal Yacht *Britannia*, while there is also a delightfully humorous cartoon entitled, *The Tea Party that nearly Was*. The en suite bathroom colour scheme is blue.

In pride of place, on the counterpane of his bed lies a tiny pot-pourri holder that was handmade by a young

BELOW: *Coaches Nos 2916 and 2922 are used by the Prince of Wales and the Duchess of Cornwall. No. 2916, fitted with a long table, is the Dining Car while No. 2922 contains the two bedrooms and bathrooms of Their Royal Highnesses. (Geoff Griffiths)*

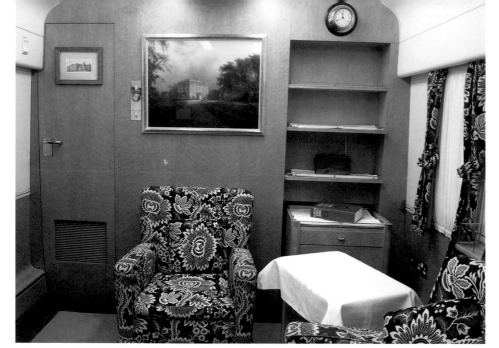

ABOVE AND RIGHT: *The Prince of Wales's sitting room, with its comfortable armchairs and his writing table with HRH's personal crested equipment. (Railcare)*

BELOW: *This charming pot-pourri holder was an unexpected gift to Prince Charles from a young girl at Haverfordwest station. She had made it herself and the Prince was so touched he has ordered that it should have pride of place on his bed ever since. (Railcare)*

girl in Wales. Prince Charles was boarding the train at Haverfordwest station when this young lady approached him and asked if she might be allowed to present him with a little gift. He was delighted and more than a little touched by this gesture and the present, which is decorated with the Prince of Wales's feathers, has remained in his sleeping compartment ever since, on his explicit orders.

A door leads into the next-door sleeping coach of the Duchess of Cornwall, which is pink in colour and

the panelling is bird's eye Maplewood to match that of the Prince's. Her Royal Highness obviously does not share her husband's taste for pictures and her carriage contains only one. When the sleeping car was being redecorated for the Duchess, she requested that blackout curtains be fitted to all the windows, as she does not like any light to filter in during the night. In daylight, the curtains are removed. Her en suite bathroom colour scheme is pink.

Although Prince Charles and his wife have separate sleeping compartments, only a partition wall divides them which is less than three inches thick. Both beds are located right in the centre of the coach, which is the most stable position, although as Chris Hillyard points out, stability is not a major problem these days as they are fitted with airbags and spring units, unlike the 1903 and even the 1940 Royal Trains where suspension did not always give the most comfortable ride.

Alongside the Duchess's bedroom is a small compartment for her dresser while adjoining Prince Charles's room is his valet's 'brushing room', where each evening he prepares the wardrobe for the next day's engagements. As His Royal Highness frequently carries out several different duties on the same day, he may have to change clothes more than once and if, for example, it involves meeting officials from different organisations or service units, he will wear the appropriate tie, so the valet keeps them with him. Quite often Prince Charles will change ties in the car en route to the next job.

It is in the valet's workroom that Prince Charles likes to leave some of his personal belongings such as his shaving brush and razor (he still uses a safety razor), his hairbrushes and cologne.

Once a year, Prince Charles, in his role as Duke of Cornwall, takes over the train to travel to the Duchy and meet as many of his tenants as he can. At various locations in the county he will invite some of them on board for luncheon or dinner in the Royal dining car, which has a central table that can seat up to 12 people and can be extended to accommodate 16 – at a pinch, or to be used, as it more usually is, as a conference table.

RIGHT: *The moment the train arrives back at Wolverton, every bedroom and bathroom is inspected and thoroughly cleaned, with all the blankets, pillows and towels replaced in time for the next journey. (Railcare)*

The Household saloons
Nos 2915, 2917, 2923 and support coaches
Nos 2920 and 2921

The dining car for the Household is exactly the same as that in any first-class schedule service: tables with seating for four people. The carriage is carpeted throughout and this gives the impression that it is slightly more luxurious than it is. The food is prepared and served by the train chef and stewards and menus have been submitted to the Palace, or Clarence House, in the case of the Prince of Wales's Household, beforehand.

Sleeping accommodation also mirrors that of a normal sleeper service, with the private secretaries having single rooms, with a washbasin, and the more junior members having to share in double bunks.

The main difference between the sleeping arrangements of the Royal Family and their staff is that the staff all have their beds running crosswise, between the rails, while the beds for the four Principals are situated lengthways, in the centre of the coach. Through trial and error it has been discovered in Victorian times, that this is the most comfortable place to position the beds, and even when the train is travelling at speed, there is far less sense of movement than if the beds were placed across the coach, as is usual with public sleeping cars. The Household does not have the choice!

The Household sleeping car is equipped with showers and lavatories, but no baths; space does not permit such luxuries.

The Queen's private secretary has the use of a small office on board and he is in constant contact with Her Majesty through the train communications system. The Queen, the Duke of Edinburgh and the Prince of Wales all have Roberts radio sets in their saloons, usually tuned to BBC Radio Four as they like to wake up in the morning and listen to the news and the 'Today' programme. There are also several television sets on the train, but as yet, reception is spasmodic when they are on the move and in certain areas, so experiments are being conducted to see if satellite receivers will improve picture quality. The train carries a video recorder so that Her Majesty can watch re-runs of any races in which one

of her horses has been running and also they have a selection of the family's favourite TV programmes that can be seen without interference. The Household saloon has a music centre installed with music occasionally piped through, and there is also a collection of CDs with a variety of music available.

On 31 August 2007, The Queen, the Duke of Edinburgh and the Prince of Wales were on board en route to London from Aberdeen station (ex-Balmoral). The occasion was to attend the anniversary memorial service to the late Diana, Princess of Wales, at the Guards Chapel in Wellington Barracks. At Armitage there was a massive signal failure and all traffic was halted for over an hour. It became obvious that they were going to have difficulties in making their scheduled time. The Train Officer spoke to his opposite number at Network Rail who promised him that once the problem was solved they would have a green light all the way to Euston. The Queen's then private secretary, Sir Robin Janvrin, was informed that the train was now running 67 minutes late and it was unlikely that they would be able to make up all that time. They were due in to London at 10.23am and the driver was given permission to exceed his normal speed for the final leg of the journey, which he actually did, once they had managed to start again, in a little over an hour, enabling the Royal Train to arrive at Euston just nine minutes late. It was a remarkable recovery and The Queen and her family were able to arrive at the memorial service exactly on time.

It is on occasions like this, thankfully very rare, that the Royal Train – and the men who run it – come into their own, proving once again that, where The Queen and her family are concerned, they are all willing to go that extra mile.

ABOVE: *Bathrooms containing baths are few and far between on the Royal Train because of the limited space. Apart from those used by the Royal Family, there are some for the Household. This one is also fitted with a shower. (RAIL magazine)*

CHAPTER 4

Royal progress

IT WAS NOT all that long ago that every time the Royal Train moved, a special pilot locomotive preceded it about half a mile ahead, making sure the road was clear and there were no obstructions.

That precaution has now been dispensed with and, because of manning shortages, a policeman is no longer stationed on every bridge under which the train passes to ensure that nothing is dropped – either deliberately or by accident. Neither is every level crossing gate manned when a Royal Train is expected to prevent any vehicle or person being stranded halfway across the line.

If all this appeared to be over compensating a little in the past, it is worth remembering that the overnight Royal Train carrying the Duke of Edinburgh on 14/15 June 1996 between Chester and London Euston, struck an individual on the track at Beeston Castle. He was killed outright and the verdict at the inquest found that it was suicide. Obviously, no blame could be attached to the driver as this was not at a level crossing but on a

RIGHT: *An unusual view from the Royal Train as it runs along the rugged Cumbrian coastline south of Whitehaven. The giant wind turbines appear to be standing guard over the rocky foreshore. (Geoff Griffiths)*

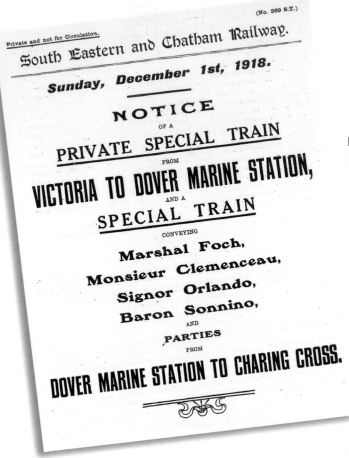

South Eastern and Chatham Railway.

Sunday, December 1st, 1918.

NOTICE

OF A

PRIVATE SPECIAL TRAIN

FROM

VICTORIA TO DOVER MARINE STATION,

AND A

SPECIAL TRAIN

CONVEYING

Marshal Foch,

Monsieur Clemenceau,

Signor Orlando,

Baron Sonnino,

AND

PARTIES

FROM

DOVER MARINE STATION TO CHARING CROSS.

lonely stretch of the railway in the dark. Nevertheless, it illustrated how important it is to be vigilant.

Looking back even further, to the 19th century, the first record of terrorism on a main line in Britain took place on 13 September 1880. A bundle of explosives was found on the track between Bushey and Watford in Hertfordshire and police investigating the affair discovered the intention was to blow up a train carrying Grand Duke Constantine of Russia. The bomb was made safe and the Duke continued his journey blissfully unaware of the near miss.

Two years later, on 2 March 1882, an attempt was made on Queen Victoria's life as she entered her carriage at Windsor station. Roderick Maclean, who had a previous conviction for attempting to wreck a train, tried to shoot her, but at his trial was found 'not guilty by reason of insanity' and later changed his plea, under the Trial of Lunatics Act 1883, to 'guilty but insane'. He was detained indefinitely in a secure mental institution.

The Prince of Wales (later King Edward VII) also survived an assassination attempt while at Brussels North Terminus station in April 1900. Police arrested another lunatic, named Sipido, and His Royal Highness continued his journey to Calais where he crossed to Dover to join the South Eastern Railway's Royal Train to Charing Cross station.

ABOVE: *A special Royal Train brought French and Italian leaders to London following the Armistice that ended the First World War in 1918.*

RIGHT: *A somewhat crowded footplate as King George V and Queen Mary joined six other people on the brand new No. 4082* **Windsor Castle** *for a short journey on 28 April 1924, from the GWR's Swindon Works to the station where the Royal couple rejoined the comfort of the Royal Train to continue to Windsor. (Patrick Kingston Collection)*

Among the more unusual aspects of Royal rail travel was one that took place in October 1840. Driver John Leonard was tasked to drive a special train from Slough to Paddington following the funeral of Princess Augusta at Windsor. He decided to give a couple of friends a lift on the footplate but was caught and admonished. In a sulk, he then proceeded to drive the train at a snail's pace all the way to London, for which he was fined 40 shillings (£2) for obstructing the line.

In 1898, Peter Peters was the stationmaster at the London & North Western Railway station at Wigan. He had failed to report for duty on 9 September, a day when the Royal Train stopped for a few minutes in the early hours of the morning at his station. He was instantly dismissed. All his efforts to obtain his job back failed and on 1 December that year he killed himself. The verdict at the inquest was: 'Suicide by cutting his throat with a razor while temporarily insane.'

Queen Victoria often had the Royal Train stopped if she wanted to see something during the journey. It is said that she frequently ordered the train to halt on top of the Wharncliffe Viaduct in Hanwell en route to Windsor so she could admire the view towards Hanwell Parish Church of St Mary.

There have been many memorable journeys by the Royal Train in the past century and a half. On Boxing Day, 26 December 1918, Field-Marshal Sir Douglas Haig was among those VIPs who welcomed the President of the United States to Britain and travelled with him in the Royal Train, sent by King George V, from Dover Marine to Charing Cross where His Majesty was waiting to offer his official greetings. Coaches supplied by the South Eastern & Chatham Railway provided this journey and it was the first visit to Britain by the American Head of State following the end of the First World War.

On 28 April 1924 The King had an opportunity to drive a locomotive. During a visit to the Great Western Railway works at Swindon accompanied by Queen Mary, His Majesty mounted the footplate and handled the controls of the giant No. 4082 *Windsor Castle*. He later expressed his satisfaction with the experience. During that same visit to Swindon, Queen Mary joined her

husband on the footplate of the locomotive, along with Sir Felix Pole, General Manager of the Great Western Railway, but there is no record of Her Majesty driving the engine. It must have been rather crowded on the footplate that day as there were no fewer than eight people, including the driver and fireman, standing in that confined space. Following the death of George V in 1936, his widow continued to use her own saloon, No. 395, which was often attached to scheduled services rather than as part of a special Royal Train.

King Edward VIII did not share his parent's love of either Sandringham or Balmoral and during his short reign of less than a year, no record exists of him using the Royal Train to travel to Norfolk, and only once to Ballater.

The most memorable journey made by Edward VIII in the Royal Train happened on 18/19 November 1936, just three weeks before his Abdication. The Train carried His Majesty from Paddington to South Wales where the first stop was at Llantwit Major, a tiny station that eventually closed under Dr Beeching's axe and happily is now reopened as part of the line between Bridgend and Cardiff Wales Airport.

The King's train consisted of two saloons, one

ABOVE: *Princesses Elizabeth and Margaret follow their grandmother, Queen Mary, at Waterloo as they wait for the departure of King George VI and Queen Elizabeth, who were travelling to Portsmouth Harbour, before sailing to Canada in May 1939. (Patrick Kingston Collection)*

LEFT: *One of the wartime LMS coaches, No. 799, built at Wolverton in 1941 and still used as part of the Royal Train until well after the end of the Second World War. (Railcare)*

ABOVE AND RIGHT: *These interior pictures show views of The Queen's sitting room and that of the Duke of Edinburgh. They are of the same vintage as LMS No. 799, but are seen as they were in the 1960s. (Railcare)*

sleeping car and a number of first-class carriages for the Household. His Majesty slept on board during the first night in Wales and the tour is mainly remembered for his famous – and often repeated – remark that 'Something must be done', referring to the appalling conditions he witnessed the people of the valleys living under following the Great Depression. Although at the time no one realised it, this was also to be the last journey by train that Edward VIII made as a reigning monarch. He had also made another famous remark when, as Prince of Wales in 1935, he joined the directors of the Great Western Railway to celebrate the company's centenary and referred to the GWR as *'The Royal Road'*, a description that has been treasured ever since.

On 6 May 1939, just four months before the outbreak of the Second World War, King George VI and Queen Elizabeth sailed for a tour of Canada. They travelled to Portsmouth in a Royal Train provided by the Southern Railway, accompanied by their daughters, Princess Elizabeth and Princess Margaret, who were going to see them off. The two Princesses travelled from Waterloo station again on 22 June to Southampton, to greet their parents on their return.

On 24 July that year, the Royal 'Firm', as King George VI liked to call his immediate family, left Portsmouth Dockyard for Victoria station in Royal saloons Nos 7930 and 7920, and corridor first No 7254 in what was the last Royal use of this stock.

The Second World War saw a huge increase in the use of the Royal Train by King George VI and his consort, Queen Elizabeth. They travelled the length and breadth

BELOW: *This photograph of five Royal Train carriages, taken in the 1960s, shows coaches from two decades. The 12-wheeled coaches were built in the 1940s and those with eight wheels in the 1950s; the saloons of Prince Charles and Princess Anne date from 1955, the Royal Dining Saloon from 1956, and the Private Secretary's Saloon from 1957. (Railcare)*

ABOVE: *Three official documents issued by British Railways on the occasion of State Visits to Britain by foreign Royalty and Heads of State, when the Royal Train was used.*

of the country boosting morale and making themselves visible to as many of their subjects as they could. For security reasons, a considerable number of Royal journeys were carried out without being publicised at the time. No fewer than 57 journeys were made on the LMSR, 44 on the LNER, 13 on the GWR and five on the Southern Railway.

In 1940/41 two new air-conditioned saloons, Nos 798 and 799, were built at Wolverton for Their Majesties and on 17/20 June 1941 they were used for the first time on the train provided by the LMSR, from London King's Cross to Newcastle, Blythe, Birtley, Sunderland, Billingham and Middlesbrough before returning to King's Cross.

On 12/13 October that year, The King and Queen again set off, this time from Euston to Crewe, Penkridge, Hereford, Monmouth and Swindon before ending their journey at Paddington. This trip was eventful in that an air raid took place at Kingham on the 22nd stopping the train for over an hour. His Majesty also had the train stopped for a time at Leominster so he could review the troops mounting a guard of honour at the station.

The sudden death of the Duke of Kent, the King's brother, who was in an RAF aircraft, which crashed in Scotland in August 1942, meant an unplanned Royal train journey from Ballater to London Euston by The King and Queen to attend HRH's funeral at Windsor.

A month later, King George VI was returning to Balmoral, via Ballater, when his train had to be held at Cheddington as an aircraft had crashed on the line ahead of them.

As has been stated, for obvious security reasons, a great deal of secrecy surrounded the rail journeys of the Royal Family in those wartime days, but records show that in one month alone, March 1943, The King and Queen travelled over 2,750 miles on three separate journeys. They visited Nottingham, Corby and Weldon, Wellingborough, Northampton, and twice travelled to Scotland, to Hawick and then to Thurso.

The following month, Their Majesties made a little bit of railway history during a 961-mile round trip from London Euston and back to London King's Cross, taking

ABOVE: *The Royal Train, its Pullman cars hauled by Rebuilt Bulleid Pacific No. 34016* **Bodmin***, waits at Dover Marine station to convey the President of Italy to London on 13 May 1958. (Patrick Kingston Collection)*

LEFT: *The station at Dover Marine was fully decked out with British and Italian flags in honour of the President's State visit. (Railcare)*

in Renfrew, Airdrie, Gleneagles, Oakley East Grange, Edinburgh and Inveresk. The historic part is contained in the report that was written after the journey when it was revealed that this was the first time that GPO telephone lines had been attached to the Royal Train.

Towards the end of the war it was revealed that The King and Queen had travelled a total of 63,385 miles in the Royal Train supporting the war effort, and in June 1944, just prior to the D-Day landings, The King made the Southern Railway Royal Train coaches available for an historic journey from London to Droxford. The passengers included Winston Churchill, General (later Field Marshal) Jan Smuts of South Africa, Mr W. L. Mackenzie King, Prime Minister of Canada, and the leader of the Free French Forces, General Charles De Gaulle.

Indeed, a number of railway saloons earned themselves temporary or lasting fame by association with

ABOVE: *Queen Elizabeth, The Queen Mother, loved travelling in the Royal Train. Here, she has just alighted from ex-GWR saloon No. 9006 at Leamington Spa on 6 November 1958.* (Patrick Kingston)

RIGHT: *In the early days of The Queen's reign the Royal Family always travelled to Wolferton, Norfolk, in the Royal Train for their Christmas holidays at Sandringham. On this occasion, 22 December 1960, BR 'Britannia' No. 70009* **Alfred the Great** *waits at London's Liverpool Street station with the ex-LNER Royal Train coaches.* (Patrick Kingston Collection)

famous people, not all of them Royal. Prominent in this field was Sir Winston Churchill's 'Special'. He was particularly fond of this saloon, a fondness he continued after the war when he needed to keep in touch with No 10 Downing Street, but not with the same urgency. Sir Winston found it difficult to relinquish the trappings of power and the railway authorities usually allowed him to continue using his saloon whenever possible. He was a difficult man to say 'No' to.

During the war, the saloons of the Royal Train had been fitted with armour plating and this remained until 1947 when, on 28–31 October, The King, Queen and Princess Elizabeth made a round trip from Paddington to several towns in Devon with their saloons being stripped of their wartime armour and also being repainted in Royal claret. It was appropriate that among the six locomotives that pulled the Royal Train during this journey, the first was named *Isambard Kingdom Brunel*.

Royalty have been inveterate followers of horseracing for generations and The Queen is no exception, as a successful owner and breeder. There are several 'immovable feasts' in the Royal calendar and The Derby at Epsom is one of them (the Cheltenham Gold Cup is

another). For years, The Queen, the late Queen Mother, the late Princess Margaret and the Duke of Edinburgh (who is not one of racing's greatest fans) used the Royal Train to travel from London to Epsom racecourse, stopping right at Tattenham Corner station in time to enjoy the afternoon's races.

The staff of the Royal Train also thoroughly enjoyed these outings, which were always purely for pleasure, with no official duties involved. Lunch on board was a relaxed affair with champagne flowing freely and by the time the train reached Epsom everyone was in the mood.

Unfortunately for The Queen and her family, the racing authorities decided to move The Derby – the 'Blue Riband' of the 'Flat' season – from Wednesday to Saturday afternoon to accommodate the television coverage for a wider audience. As The Queen is at Windsor at weekends and it was found to be more convenient and less expensive to travel by road, the Royal Train is no longer required for this unique and happy Royal occasion. When she was at Buckingham Palace during the week, the Royal Train had been used from London's Victoria station.

It was a special year in 1953 for The Queen, of course, as she was crowned Elizabeth II in Westminster Abbey on 2 June. Four days later, on 6 June, she and Prince Philip travelled from Euston to Tattenham Corner in a Royal Train provided by the then nationalised British Railways (Southern Region). Four Pullman cars were utilised: *Isle of Thanet, Aries, Phoenix* (for Her Majesty) and *Minerva*, pulled by 'Schools' class locomotives Nos 30915 *Brighton* and 30922 *Marlborough*. It was an historic day for the famous Derby as the race was won for the first time by Britain's favourite jockey (Sir) Gordon Richards riding 'Pinza'. It was a fitting end to an exciting week as Britain threw off the last vestiges of the early post-war austerity.

For the Coronation itself, guests of The Queen, from all over the world, started arriving in Britain and the Royal Train was brought into use to transport many of them several days before the ceremony itself. Travelling from Dover Marine to London Victoria, one train alone comprised 12 separate Pullman coaches: *Isle of Thanet,*

Penelope, Rosemary, Chloria, Zenobia, Aries, Aurelia, Philomel, Onyx, Phoenix, Casandra and *Minerva*. The engines were 'Britannias' Nos 70004 *William Shakespeare* and 70030 *William Wordsworth*.

In April 1957, an unusual occurrence delayed the Royal Train as The Queen set off to undertake engagements in Worcestershire. Leaving Windsor & Eton station at 10pm on the Monday the Royal Train of eleven coaches was hauled by two 'Castle' class engines. Around midnight the train was running at an unaccustomed slow speed and word came back that two ponies had jumped their fence ahead on the track and decided to trot in front of the Royal Train. A message was passed ahead to close a crossing. This was done and several people, who thought they were cowboys, did a 'rodeo' act to catch the ponies, using ropes and anything else they could lay their hands on. Knowing Her Majesty's love of horses it would indeed have been tragic if the

driver had not seen these animals and been able to adjust his speed accordingly. However, they were rescued and safely returned to their field, and the train proceeded on its way to the siding where it was stabled for the night. The Queen was kept informed of the incident, as she is whenever anything unusual occurs, and she expressed her quiet satisfaction that all had been well in the end.

As far as Her Majesty is concerned, there is little doubt that the journey she made between 13 and 15 October 1965 must have been tinged with more than a little sadness. This was the final journey by the Royal Train from Ballater and it travelled via Dalmally and Taynuilt to Alyth Junction. It was truly the end of an age that had seen Emperors, Kings, Queens, Princes and Princesses, Sultans, Shahs and Tsars, all being transported to and from the British monarch's Highland home for more than a hundred years.

On the occasion of the Investiture of Prince Charles as Prince of Wales on 1 July 1969, the Royal Family boarded the Royal Train at Euston and travelled overnight to Caernarvon via Crewe and Bangor. A small faction of Welsh nationalists who opposed the ceremony, caused delays at Crewe and elsewhere along the route when suspected 'explosive devices' were discovered on the line. None was detonated, but a short distance from Bangor, signal wires and telephone cables had been cut and extra security was necessary when the Royal Train, whose passengers included The Queen, the Queen Mother, the Duke of Edinburgh, Princess Margaret and Princess Anne, was stabled for the night in sidings near Menai Bridge, overlooking the Isle of Anglesey.

However, no incidents occurred near the train and as the television coverage began early the next morning, the BBC had installed two temporary television sets on board so that The Queen and her family could watch the morning's events unfold.

Before lunch on 1 July, the Royal party decided to leave the Royal Train and visit the nearby home of Sir Michael Duff, Lord Lieutenant of Caernarvonshire,

BELOW: On 1 July 1969 a Guard of Honour parades to welcome all the Royal Family to Caernarvon, where the Investiture of Prince Charles as Prince of Wales was to take place. Here, the Royal Train is seen having arrived at the 'Ferodo Platform' which was constructed at the well-known engineering works specially for the occasion. (Railcare)

BELOW: *The luncheon menu on one of the 'special trains' which ran from King's Cross to York for the wedding of the Duke and Duchess of Kent in June 1961. Non-Royal guests were charged £1 for the meal!*

incidentally the Godfather of Her Majesty's brother-in-law, the Earl of Snowdon, who was organising the ceremony at Caernarvon Castle.

Unfortunately, there was no road access to the sidings (there often isn't for obvious reasons), so BR arranged for a special 'Royal' train consisting of a diesel locomotive and an inspection saloon to carry them to the nearest road crossing three quarters of a mile away, where they transferred to a fleet of motor cars for the remainder of the journey. The Royal Family were highly amused at the 'unique' Royal Train and impressed by the imagination and efficiency of British Railways.

When the 150th anniversary of the Great Western Railway Act 1835 was marked on 26 July 1985, The Queen named a diesel locomotive No 47620 *Windsor Castle* at Paddington station, continuing a Royal tradition. But it was her late mother, Queen Elizabeth, who made history by becoming the first member of the Royal Family to name a modern traction locomotive (diesel or electric) when she christened Class 47 diesel No 47541 *The Queen Mother* at Aberdeen on 20 October 1982. It was as far back as 15 November 1950 that The Queen (as Princess Elizabeth) named the last

'Castle' class 4-6-0, No.7037 *Swindon* when she also rode on the footplate of 'Star' class 4-6-0 No.4057 *Princess Elizabeth* during a visit to the Swindon Works.

Another high spot in the Train's life occurred on 8 June 1961 when HRH the Duke of Kent married Miss Katherine Worsley at York Minster, and a very large gathering of Royalty and non-Royal guests included the cream of the establishment of this and many other countries. Special trains ran from King's Cross to York returning from Malton where the reception was held at the bride's former home.

8 June 1961

SMOKED RIVER TROUT

* * *

ROAST TURKEY

CHIPOLATA – BREAD SAUCE

GARDEN PEAS

CHATEAU & PARSLEY POTATOES

* * *

STRAWBERRIES WITH LIQUEUR

WHIPPED FRESH CREAM

* * *

CHEESE – SALAD – BISCUITS

* * *

COFFEE

ABOVE: *One of the most famous locomotives in the world, ex-LNER No. 4472* **Flying Scotsman***, is seen leaving Stratford (Low Level) for North Woolwich, taking the Queen Mother to open the North Woolwich Station Museum on 20 November 1984. (Patrick Kingston)*

The former LNER Royal train was strengthened considerably and a second restaurant car was included because of the large number of passengers on the train.

Apart from short journeys for Royal funerals this was probably the greatest number of Royalty and VIPs ever to travel together in the one train.

The non-Royal guests on the special trains paid £1 per head each for the luncheon and dinner (Royalty was not required to pay) and the dinner menu, which was served to several hundred guests, shows that, as with all Royal menus it was a simple English meal of excellent quality.

A new Royal dining car was built in the 1950s and had a novel feature in so far as the saloon could be made large or small at will by removable partitions, while the table was specially made to be extendable. For small parties an intimacy could be created by this means with the décor looking exactly the same as when expanded to the full. Car No 499 was a standard vehicle of 64ft 6in, and was an eight-wheeler, and the saloon included a pantry, kitchen, staff compartment and staff toilet.

It weighed 43 tons but was by no means the heaviest vehicle in the train. In all there were eleven vehicles which were 743ft in length and weighed 498 tons.

Among the many significant journeys the Royal Train has undertaken, one of the least enjoyable was on 23/24 January 1989, when the Prince of Wales in a six-car assembly travelled from King's Lynn to Glasgow Central, stopping at Lockerbie on the way. There, HRH visited the site of the air crash caused by a terrorist

BELOW: *Queen Elizabeth, The Queen Mother, was delighted to be asked to travel to Aberdeen on 20 October 1982 when she named Class 47 No. 47541* **The Queen Mother**. *It was the first diesel locomotive to be named by a member of the Royal Family. (Patrick Kingston)*

ABOVE AND RIGHT:
Appropriate locomotive naming ceremonies are all part of the Sovereign's public duties and when her Majesty was asked to take part in one at Worcester Shrub Hill on 10 November 1989 it was a double pleasure as No. 47528 was to be named **The Queen's Own Mercian Yeomanry***. (Colin J. Marsden)*

ABOVE: *On 28 June 1991 The Queen named InterCity Class 91 electric locomotive No. 91029* **Queen Elizabeth II** *at London's King's Cross to mark the launch of the East Coast Main Line electric service. Surely the only time carpeted steps have been laid at the driver's cab door? (Colin J. Marsden)*

detonating a bomb on the aircraft (Pan Am Flight 103) on 21 December 1988, killing all 259 passengers and crew on board and a further eleven people on the ground.

A happier occasion was celebrated in 2002, the Golden Jubilee of Her Majesty. She and Prince Philip carried out a number of Jubilee tours covering a total of 7,134 miles in all. Between 30 April and 2 May they travelled from Euston to Falmouth, St Austell and Exeter St David's in coaches numbers: 2921, 2903, 2904, 2918, 2923, 2917, 2915 and 2920. Appropriately, they were pulled by Nos 47798 *Prince William* and 47799 *Prince Henry*, both of which, as Class 47 locomotives, have now been retired from Royal service and replaced by the new Class 67 engines. After withdrawal, No 47798 was specially repainted in Royal Claret livery at Wolverton for presentation by EWS to the National Collection, in fully operational main line condition. However, EWS was naturally opposed to the National Railway Museum then wishing to repaint it again, into standard BR blue, and it has since been passed on loan to a rival company, West Coast Railway at Carnforth. No 47799 is stored, its future uncertain.

ABOVE: *The Queen leaves the Royal Train at Euston station on 13 June 2002 at the conclusion of the Golden Jubilee tour of Wales. She holds a crystal paperweight, presented by Chris Hillyard on behalf of the Royal Train staff, which commemorated 160 years to the very day of the Royal Train Service. (Mick Foster)*

LEFT: *The Queen Mother thanks Chris Hillyard as Prince Philip waits patiently. This was an historic occasion as it was the last time the Royal Train ran to Tattenham Corner station for the Epsom Derby – 7 June 1997. (Mick Foster)*

The Royal Family's love of trains

ABOVE AND RIGHT: *The Queen and the Duke of Edinburgh enjoy heritage steam on a day out on the Bodmin & Wenford Railway on 8 June 2000. Their train was hauled by 0-6-0ST* **Ugly** *and ex-GWR 0-6-0PT No. 9682. (Bob Sweet)*

ABOVE:
Her Majesty is obviously enjoying the ride at Exbury Gardens travelling in the cab of a brand-new steam locomotive she had just named **Marilioo** *on 3 May 2008. (James Bunch)*

ABOVE: *The Prince of Wales and the Duchess of Cornwall meet some of the volunteers at the Grand Opening of the new Wharf station at the Talyllyn Railway on 13 July 2005. (Bob Sweet)*

LEFT: *Prince Philip on the footplate of steam engine No. 7820* **Dinmore Manor** *at Minehead, on the West Somerset Railway, on 1 November 2002. Unusually, the Royal Train travelled the length of the heritage railway. It was headed by Class 47 No. 47798* **Prince William.** *(Alan Grieve)*

ABOVE: *There is no more majestic sight than a magnificent steam locomotive in pristine condition as proved when No. 6233* **Duchess of Sutherland** *hauled the Royal Train for the Golden Jubilee tour of Wales in 2002 and also (above) in March 2005 on the occasion of the visit of the Prince of Wales to the Settle & Carlisle Railway in Cumbria when he rode on the footplate. (Geoff Griffiths)*

In June 2002, The Queen and Prince Philip left Euston in a six-coach train for North Wales where the first station on the Isle of Anglesey has a name longer than the platform: Llanfairpwllgwyngyllgogerychwyndrobwyllllantysiliogogogoch (or Llanfair PG as the locals know it), at the start of a Jubilee tour of Wales. Class 47 Nos 47787 *Windsor Castle* (name applied to this locomotive in 2002, as previously carried by No 47620/47835), and 47798 *Prince William* drew them, but between Llanfair PG, Llandudno Junction and Dolau, in North Wales, they were hauled by No 6233, a former LMS steam engine named *Duchess of Sutherland*, over some of the most spectacular countryside in the Principality. For the South Wales section of the tour they were headed again by *Prince William* and *Windsor Castle* taking them from Llanelli to Port Talbot Parkway, Bridgend, Newport and Cardiff Central, from where they returned to London Euston.

The Prince of Wales is particularly fond of steam travel and on two occasions his train has been hauled by a steam locomotive on the main line. There are still quite a number left in the country, many of which have been restored from near wrecks including those rescued from a railway 'graveyard' in Barry Docks. *Duchess of Sutherland* is one such case, having spent many years on open air static display in a Butlin's holiday camp. Her restoration took several years and cost over £500,000, which included a grant from the Heritage Lottery Fund. Whenever Prince Charles travels on a steam-hauled train he likes to mount the footplate to experience the thrill that all young boys used to dream about.

Even today there are still so many enthusiasts about that whenever the Royal Train is scheduled to pass a particular point, you can guarantee that hundreds will turn out to see her, and if a steam engine is attached, the watching crowd can run into thousands.

When the Prince of Wales is using the Royal Train, Geoff Griffiths at EWS, which has been operating the Royal Train since 1996, will attach a couple of Red Dragon Welsh flags to the front of the locomotives. As a gesture to the Principality, he has also printed the timetable in Welsh as well as English on more than one occasion. As Prince Charles employs an assistant private secretary who is a native born Welsh speaker, it is as well that the timetable is word perfect.

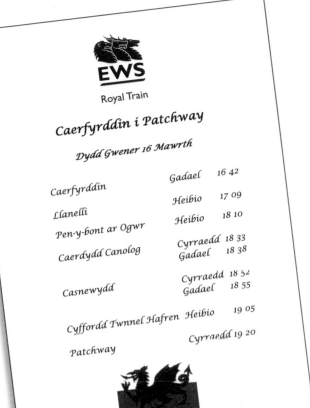

EWS

Royal Train

Caerfyrddin i Patchway

Dydd Gwener 16 Mawrth

Caerfyrddin	Gadael	16 42
Llanelli	Heibio	17 09
Pen-y-bont ar Ogwr	Heibio	18 10
Caerdydd Canolog	Cyrraedd	18 33
	Gadael	18 38
Casnewydd	Cyrraedd	18 52
	Gadael	18 55
Cyffordd Twnnel Hafren	Heibio	19 05
Patchway	Cyrraedd	19 20

English Welsh & Scottish Railway Ltd

ABOVE LEFT: *Geoff Griffiths provided the first Royal Train timetable in Welsh when the Prince of Wales travelled from Carmarthen to (Bristol) Patchway via Llanelli, Bridgend, Cardiff Central, Newport and Severn Tunnel Junction. (Geoff Griffiths)*

LEFT AND ABOVE: *When Prince Charles is using the Royal Train the locomotive is decorated with two Red Dragon Welsh flags. Here, No. 67006* **Royal Sovereign** *is seen at Llandudno Junction on 7 June 2007. (Geoff Griffiths)*

CHAPTER 5

The cost and value

S INCE 1 April 1997 (All Fool's Day), the Royal Household has been responsible for the costs of all Royal rail and air travel. Prior to this, every penny was paid by the Department of Transport. Not that anything has really changed; it is all a matter of accounting. The difference is that instead of the department paying the costs directly to the railway companies, they now provide the necessary funds to the Palace who *then* settle the bills themselves. The main objectives in transferring the expenditure to the Household were to improve accountability and to make the accounts more transparent.

The Department of Transport still provides the money through the Royal Travel Grant-in-Aid, but now the Royal Household is solely responsible for Royal travel expenditure, instead of the various Government departments, as in the past.

Since the Royal Household assumed control of the Royal Train finances, there has been a more accountable

RIGHT: *This dramatic picture, taken from the rear coaches of the Royal Train on 1 March 2006, the first day of a new financial year, shows icy conditions as the train approaches Wrexham. (Geoff Griffiths)*

set of management arrangements. It has become a business with a clear and identifiable commercial role with a focussed attack on basic costs that has provided the foundation for its present success.

Although the Train is very popular with the Royal Family and remains a sophisticated and ultra-comfortable, if conventional, way to travel, helicopters and fixed-wing aircraft have in the main replaced the train for shorter journeys, being faster and more economical to operate. The completion of the motorway system such as the M4 and M5 means that the Prince of Wales can drive from London to South Wales or his properties in the Duchy of Cornwall almost as fast as

travelling by train, and certainly far cheaper.

Ten years ago, the Train was used for a total of 24 journeys with an average distance per trip of around 550 miles. In 2007 the Train carried out 17 journeys with an average distance of 655 miles. In the same period, members of the Royal Family made 49 journeys by scheduled train (one more than the previous year) with an average distance of 130 miles per journey as opposed to 165 miles per journey in 2006.

The Queen and the Duke of Edinburgh used the Train on four occasions during the year. On 24/25 May, they travelled from Euston to Blackburn to attend a Duchy of Lancaster reception (Her Majesty is, of course, the Duke of Lancaster), as well as several other engagements in the area including visiting the town centre to see the new developments. The Privy Purse was charged a total of £15,156 for the rail travel and £7,434 when Her Majesty and His Royal Highness flew on to Aberdeen by a BAe 146 of No 32 (The Royal) Squadron.

The Queen, accompanied by the Duke of Edinburgh, again used the Train when she visited the Eden Project in Cornwall on 31 May/1 June, leaving from Euston at 23.59 and travelling overnight to St Austell at a cost of

£13,390. They returned to Northolt by fixed-wing aircraft costing £3,924.

The most expensive rail journey involving The Queen and the Duke of Edinburgh was on 16/17 November when they travelled between Euston, Arlesey, Sandy and Windsor. The Queen opened the Samuel Whitbread Community College and visited the Defence Intelligence and Security Centre among her other engagements, and the journey cost £21,308.

The final train journey by The Queen and the Duke of

BELOW: *Snow in March is not unheard of in Wales, but usually St David's Day, on the first day of the month, is more Spring-like, with daffodils in full bloom; not in 2006 however, as the Royal Train approaches Newtown in Powys behind silver-liveried No. 67029. (Geoff Griffiths)*

ABOVE: *Locomotive No. 67029 at Coventry on 1 March 2006 en route to Machynlleth, heading empty stock from Wolverton, to collect the Duke of Edinburgh and take him to Wrexham. (Geoff Griffiths)*

Edinburgh in the financial year ending 31 March 2007 was from Euston to Brighton and Windsor. The object of the journey was to enable Her Majesty to visit the Theatre Royal, the Jubilee Library, the Pavilion Theatre and to carry out other official engagements. This was the second most expensive rail journey for The Queen as it cost a total of £19,271.

So the overall cost of transporting The Queen and the Duke of Edinburgh, including their Households and their overnight accommodation, was a modest £69,125 for the entire year.

The Prince of Wales used the Royal Train to travel from Aberdeen to Lincoln on the 2/3 May at a cost of £24,354 to visit the city centre and Lincoln Cathedral.

With the Duchess of Cornwall, which meant an extra coach on the Train, he travelled from Kemble (the nearest station to Highgrove) on an overnight trip on 29/30 May to Dumfries, where they carried out a number of engagements including visiting Borders General Hospital, Kinloch Castle, attending a reception at the Scottish Parliament, and His Royal Highness gave a speech at the Heritage Cities Organisation of World North West Regional Conference. The cost: £20,905 for rail travel plus a further £7,695 to take them back to Ballater.

Their Royal Highnesses again joined the Royal Train on 6 July to travel from Kemble, this time to Edinburgh, where Prince Charles attended the opening of a

Memorial Garden to his grandmother, Queen Elizabeth, The Queen Mother in the Royal Botanic Gardens, after which he joined other members of the Royal Family at the Palace of Holyroodhouse for the annual Order of the Thistle Service. This two-day journey cost £20,737.

The following month, the Royal couple used the Train on 12/13 July travelling overnight from Euston to Hornbeam Park in Yorkshire for engagements at the Royal Yorkshire Show and at Royal Hall in Harrogate. The costs of this trip were £16,039 in addition to £8,980 incurred when an aircraft was chartered for the return journey.

Prince Charles again used the Train in November 2006 to travel from Euston to Newcastle on 7/8 where he and the Duchess visited Newcastle United Football Club. The cost was £16,740, but the expense of chartering a helicopter for the return journey nearly equalled that of the Train at £12,585.

The least expensive train journey undertaken by the Prince of Wales and the Duchess of Cornwall had nothing to do with the Royal Train and was undertaken on a private service abroad. It was a chartered train they used during their visit to the United States in January 2007, when, on the 28th they experienced the joys of American railways travelling from Philadelphia to New York at a cost of £3,870.

Back home, Kemble, arguably the most frequently used station for the Royal Train apart from Euston and Windsor, saw Prince Charles travelling overnight to Carlisle on 4/5 February, £18,696, while in March 2007, His Royal Highness left Euston just before midnight on the 15th for the familiar journey to Carmarthen to visit the National Botanic Garden of Wales and to carry out other engagements as part of British Tourism Week 2007. By the time the Train had deposited him back at Patchway, en route to his home at Highgrove, the cost had reached £22,548.

We have not noted the train journeys by scheduled services as all of these are under the £10,000 limit revealed in the Royal Household accounts, but those we have mentioned give a reasonable idea of the extent of the use of the Royal Train in an average year and the expense involved.

When Buckingham Palace, through its Director of

Royal Travel, decides a Royal Train journey is required, Geoff Griffiths at EWS is asked to provide an estimate of the total cost. He works out the hire charge for each locomotive and the amount of fuel that will be required. Then the number of engine drivers that will be necessary and how much they cost and the number and charges applied to the engineers who will accompany the train. Network Rail planning and track access fees have to be worked out and Railcare charges and those that have to be paid to Rail Gourmet for the chefs, stewards and food and drink provided.

As each journey is different, these estimates have to be planned every time, with allowances made for whether an overnight stop is required and the distance

ABOVE: *The Prince of Wales and the Duchess of Cornwall were on board the Train hauled by No. 67006 on 13 July 2006 when this photograph was taken at Doncaster. The Royal couple had travelled overnight from Euston to Hornbeam Park, Yorkshire, for a number of engagements at the Royal Yorkshire Show. (Geoff Griffiths)*

OPPOSITE TOP: *The only time the Royal Train has been used by someone outside the Royal Family was on 16 May 1998, when Cherie Blair, wife of the then Prime Minister, invited the wives of world leaders attending the G8 Heads of Government Conference in Britain, to join her for a day trip. (Mick Foster)*

BELOW: *The Queen and the Duke of Edinburgh were on board the Royal Train seen here at Grantham, Lincolnshire, on 17 November 2006. (Geoff Griffiths)*

to be travelled. The Palace pays for every mile. British Transport Police are asked for their estimate and this will include the number of officers required to travel and those involved in security checks at either end and at the overnight stabling point. Overtime can be a major element in these costs.

Once the overall estimate has been worked out, it is submitted to Buckingham Palace for approval and again, once the journey has been completed, the figures are updated to take into account the actual costs. An invoice is sent to the Palace for settlement and after it has been scrutinised and paid by the Keeper of the Privy Purse, the third party suppliers receive their money from EWS. It sounds like a complicated method but experience has shown that the Train is run at minimal cost and EWS provide an efficient and economic service to the Royal Family.

It is impossible to justify the expense of running the

Royal Train without taking into consideration the savings made by not using alternative means of transport. As most of today's journeys are of overnight duration, it would involve finding, and paying for, secure and suitable accommodation for, say, The Queen and Prince Philip, and their staff. As there are not all that many private houses available these days that are suitable for providing accommodation for members of the Royal Family, hotels would have to be found and this alone would cause severe difficulties that the management might find insurmountable. They would have to vet their other guests, which would embarrass and inconvenience them; they would, in all probability, have to turn away paying guests who had already booked and paid for their accommodation. Security would be a major issue, as it is whenever a member of the Royal Family is staying in a public place and the police authorities would need extra manpower in order

to ensure that The Queen, or whoever it was, was totally safe. The cost of these additional measures would be considerably more than the cost of running the Royal Train – and not necessarily more efficient.

In all the accusations of profligate spending that have been levelled at the Royal Family, no-one could honestly say they have been wasteful in terms of the Royal Train. When you realise that the saloons of King Edward VII lasted over half a century and were still being used at the outbreak of the Second World War, while King George V's bath on board was used from 1915 until 1941, nobody could say the Royal Family has indulged itself at public expense.

In 2001, The Queen and Prince Philip made history by travelling on the 09.45 train from London Paddington to Chippenham in Wiltshire and saved a considerable amount of public money by doing so. There were more than a hundred other commuters on the train, but Her Majesty and His Royal Highness arrived with little fuss and took their seats in a specially reserved first-class carriage. They were travelling on return tickets that had been bought by their staff for £39.70 each: a special Apex fare when bought a week in advance. The visit to Chippenham was to undertake official engagements and the Royal Train would normally have been used for such occasions, but this time an eagle-eyed member of the Royal Household spotted the bargain price and the fact that the train times fitted in perfectly with The Queen's schedule. As most journeys by the Royal Train cost over £30,000 each, it was estimated that Her Majesty saved well over £29,000 on this occasion. It has not been revealed if The Queen and Prince Philip were asked to show their tickets to the train manager, or if they made use of the complimentary at-seat trolley service that operated as normal during the journey. The train did arrive at Chippenham exactly on time! It was a perfect example of practicality winning over protocol.

RIGHT: In 2001 The Queen and the Duke of Edinburgh made a little bit of railway history when they joined more than 100 other passengers on a normal schedule service from London Paddington to Chippenham in Wiltshire. Their first class tickets cost just £39.70 each! On another occasion, on 3 March 2000, The Queen is seen alighting from a scheduled Virgin Trains service. (Bob Sweet)

Although it would be impracticable to allow members of the public to wander through the Royal Train, as they can at Buckingham Palace, Windsor Castle and now, Clarence House, if it were possible, it would certainly demonstrate that The Queen adheres to what has been described as 'good old-fashioned Hanoverian housekeeping policies' in regard to her train.

Her Majesty will not allow any unnecessary expense and when and if replacements for curtains, carpets and furniture are required, she has to be convinced that the old ones do not have a few more years left in them before she agrees to money being spent.

Obviously, because the train does not

ABOVE: *Ex-GWR 'King' class No. 6024* **King Edward I** *heads the Royal Train, adorned with the Prince of Wales's three feathers, on 10 June 2008. It pauses at Arley on the Severn Valley Railway, en route from Kidderminster to Bridgnorth, watched by a plain-clothes police officer. This was the first time the Royal Train was steam-hauled on a heritage railway. The two previous occasions, to the West Somerset Railway and Paignton & Dartmouth Railway, the train was diesel-hauled, while other heritage railway visits have used the railway's own passenger coaches. (Patrick Kingston)*

carry out anywhere near the same amount of journeys as scheduled services, the interiors do not get as much hard wear, and therefore, do not require decorating and/or replacing with the same regularity. Chris Hillyard and his small team at Wolverton examine every inch of the Royal coaches the moment they return to the depot and so any minor repairs are attended to immediately before they become major faults.

After every trip, any complaints or other comments by the client, usually made through the Director of Royal Travel, are examined by the executives involved in running the Royal Train: the Account Manager, the Train Officer, the Catering Manager and ultimately, if the comment concerns the interior of the Train or the comfort of the passengers, the Special Vehicle Manager at Wolverton, Chris Hillyard.

And each of these gentlemen takes a personal pride in his job, so on the rare occasions when there is a problem, it receives immediate attention. It does not matter how minute the problem may appear to the layman's eye; it could be simply a badly folded napkin, a crew member wearing an unofficial tie, or the driver not bringing the train to a halt with his usual smoothness, everything is noted and goes into a final report that follows every journey. In that way, they are able to ensure that it does not happen again. There is only one standard when dealing with Royalty: perfection.

To the everyday traveller, this might seem petty and unnecessary, but The Queen and her family rely on the Train to carry them to and from their official duties with the minimum of fuss and exactly on time – each journey. Her Majesty regards punctuality as being of prime importance. She hates being late for anything, and excuses are not tolerated.

One mixed blessing with the present Royal Train is that, although it is now able to travel at speeds up to 100mph compared to 70mph before 1977, the increased speed necessitates more maintenance on the coaches than previously. The locomotives can cope easily with the faster speeds; in fact, they could achieve 125mph, just like the daily high-speed intercity services, but it is the coaches that require them to restrict their speed.

It is worth noting that in 1985 InterCity Special Trains was set up to operate a number of VIP trains and to

ABOVE: *The Prince of Wales and the Duchess of Cornwall spent the day at the Severn Valley Railway on 10 June 2008 when His Royal Highness unveiled a plaque commemorating their visit. (Bob Sweet)*

LEFT: *Nothing is wasted or thrown away on the Royal Train! Some of the soft furnishings are decades old and this pre-1948 LMS under-blanket is still being used in the Household sleeping car. (RAIL magazine)*

manage the Royal Train. Between its start-up year and 1994, when the company sold off its assets, including six Class 47 diesel-electric locomotives and 200 coaches, plus a number of profitable contracts such as that of running the 'Venice Simplon-Orient-Express', InterCity always managed to show a modest profit, and their proud boast was that the Royal Train never made a loss.

The Royal Family's love affair with rail travel is demonstrated by the fact that 2008 looks like being one of the busiest ever for the Royal Train with no fewer than ten journeys planned for the first six months alone.

CHAPTER 6

Early days

T O MANY people today, the most common image of Queen Victoria is of a short, stout, formidable figure who rarely smiled and who was only seen wearing widow's weeds. What few realise is that until her beloved husband, Prince Albert, died she was a happy carefree young woman who enjoyed trying new things, but only if they were first suggested by him.

Such was the case for her first journey by rail in 1842. Albert had already made several train journeys alone before he managed to persuade her that she should try this new form of transport which, he said, she would find much more convenient than the horsedrawn carriages she had been used to.

As is the custom today, Her Majesty had become used to spending weekends at Windsor Castle returning to Buckingham Palace on Monday to start the working week. A century ago, the journey from Windsor to London in the summer was hot and dusty as there were no main roads and when the Queen's carriage, as was

RIGHT: *Ex-LNER B2 class 4-6-0 No. 61671* **Royal Sovereign** *passes Red Hall signalbox south of Hatfield on 9 February 1953, travelling from Wolferton to London, King's Cross. (Patrick Kingston Collection)*

ABOVE: *Even the notices announcing the arrangements of carriages on the Royal Train were colourful and tastefully decorated. This one, issued by the London and North Western Railway, was the formal document relating to Queen Victoria's journey from Windsor to Holyhead.*

often the case, was forced to stop or slow down en route, it was besieged by passers-by who wanted to see her at close quarters. Victoria hated this close contact and when Prince Albert, who she had married in February 1840, suggested an alternative that would mean no-one could get too close – and which would also shorten the journey time considerably – she cautiously agreed to try it. Albert had himself first travelled by train nearly three years earlier, on 14 November 1839, when, accompanied by Prince Ernst of Saxe-Coburg-Gotha, who acted as an intermediary, His Royal Highness journeyed from Paddington to Slough and thence to Windsor in order to propose to his future bride.

Victoria may have been the first reigning British monarch to travel by rail, but her relative, King Frederick IV of Prussia, was the first reigning monarch of any country to use a train in Britain when he travelled on the same route from London to Slough in

January 1842, five months before Victoria's trip, in order to attend the christening of the Prince of Wales at Windsor Castle.

It is worth looking at the GWR Royal saloon used in those days. It was described as a broad gauge posting carriage with clerestory (domed cathedral type) roof. There were three compartments, the two at either end being 4ft 6in long and 9ft wide, with end windows. The centre section, reserved for the Royal passenger exclusively, was 12ft in length, 8ft wide and 6ft 6in high. The lavish interior was fitted out by the noted upholsterer, Mr Webb, whose premises were at Old Bond Street, London and it contained crimson and white silk hangings and sofas in the style of Louis XIV. The floors were covered in chequered matting, there was a rosewood table, and the partitions were decorated with paintings of the four seasons by Parris. The outside of the coaches were painted in rich dark chocolate brown (the dark purple colour known as

Royal Claret was not adopted until many years later).

Following that first journey by the King of Prussia, the carriage continued to be used until late in the 1850s, after which it was converted into a first-class coach and was eventually broken up in the 1870s.

At the time Queen Victoria made her first railway journey, there was, of course, no railway station at Windsor itself, and the Queen would oppose the building of one for some years on the grounds that it would bring the 'wrong sort of people' to Windsor, and the station would infringe on her privacy. She was supported in her opposition by nearby Eton College for the same elitist reasons. In fact, the Provost of Eton opposed the building of any station within three miles of the college on the grounds that it might encourage his pupils to be 'whisked off to London and be injurious to their morals.' He also ordered a fence to be erected on each side of the railway at Slough to keep his pupils out. That the Provost was successful, was emphasised when he forced his conditions into the 1835 Act of Parliament which incorporated the Great Western Railway.

So for this first history-making Royal trip, on the morning of Monday, 13 June 1842, Her Majesty proceeded by carriage from Windsor Castle to Slough railway station which was to take longer than the subsequent rail journey to London. Queen Victoria was just 22 years old and for her this was an adventure almost comparable today with Elizabeth II going into space!

The Great Western Railway, which ran services on this line, knew what a huge public relations boost and subsequent commercial advantage Royal patronage would bring, and they had provided an elaborate waiting room at Slough station for the Queen to rest in before boarding the train. They had also built a special Royal carriage to convey Her Majesty the 18 miles to London. It was 21ft long and divided into three separate compartments.

In addition to Her Majesty's carriage there were two others for members of her entourage, three trucks for the luggage and a second class brake carriage. A brand-new steam engine, just a month old, called *Phlegethon*, was used to pull the carriages, with the GWR's famous engineering genius, Isambard Kingdom Brunel, the man most closely identified with rail travel in Britain, spending the entire trip on the footplate.

Brunel was accompanied by his Locomotive Superintendent, Daniel Gooch, who had joined the GWR in 1837 and who was to become Chairman of the Board in 1865. He also became a Member of Parliament and was knighted after laying the first transatlantic cable. In charge of the Royal Train was Jim Hurst, the first man to be employed by the GWR as a locomotive driver and he remained their number one driver for many years. He wore a distinctive white corduroy uniform and was paid an extra sovereign for this, and every other Royal Train he drove, including those conveying Tsars, Archdukes, Duchesses and Shahs.

Someone else who insisted on travelling on the engine was the Queen's personal footman, who, for some reason, felt his presence alone guaranteed Her Majesty's safety. What he hadn't realised was that the footplate of a steam engine was a very dirty place and he had not bothered to change out of his court uniform of scarlet coat and white breeches. By the time the train reached London, the man was covered in coal dust and he there and then decided that enough was enough and never travelled on the footplate again. Thereafter, the railway company, in an effort to shield Royal eyes from anything as distressing as black coal dust, sometimes painted the top layers white, not, it should be added, on the orders of Her Majesty.

The senior members of the Royal Household, who had tried to persuade The Queen not to try this newfangled way of travelling, hated the experience, but she was thrilled. 'I am quite charmed by it,' she wrote later that day to her favourite uncle, King Leopold of The Belgians, 'By railroad from Windsor in half an hour, free from dust and heat.' If the GWR had only been aware of this endorsement at the time it would have been worth its weight in gold.

The journey from Slough to Paddington, which was not the magnificent station we know today; that was not built until twelve years later in 1854, when Prince Albert and the King of Portugal also performed a joint opening ceremony of the magnificent Great Western Hotel – now the Hilton – but a rudimentary collection

of sheds at Bishop's Road a short distance away. This first Paddington station was formed with a single platform with the south face for departing trains and the north for arrivals. The station had been hastily thrown together and was immediately south of the Paddington arm of the Grand Junction Canal. It took exactly 22 minutes and 30 seconds for the 18 miles to the arches of Bishop's Bridge, which formed the GWR station offices, at an average speed of 48.66mph. This was the fastest any sovereign had ever travelled before and even the daring Prince Albert was constrained to request the 'conductor' not to travel so fast.

In fact, this journey was among the fastest Victoria would ever make in her lifetime. The only other times a train carrying her would ever exceed this speed were her funeral train bringing her coffin from London to Windsor in 1901, and an occasion in June 1846, when the engine of a Royal Train failed at Slough and Her Majesty's train was pulled by the only other engine available, a 2-4-0 goods engine named *Buffalo*. The driver was a 26-year-old man named John Hastle and he, in the excitement of the moment, exceeded the company's speed limit and drove at over 60mph. The directors were furious and

docked him a sovereign from his wages for giving Queen Victoria such a bumpy ride.

Throughout her life, as much as Victoria enjoyed train travel, she refused to allow any of her trains to travel at more than 40mph in daylight and 30mph at night. It is said that she had a special signal installed on the roof of one of her carriages so she could instruct the driver to slow down if she felt he was going too fast. Sketches of the GWR's 1851 Royal Saloon depict such a device which was to be observed by a second train guard, riding on the locomotive footplate looking backwards along the train's length and relaying Her Majesty's instruction to the driver. Not a task to be enjoyed on a cold winter's day. It has never been established if this signal was merely cosmetic, or indeed, if it did exist, or if it did, if the driver ever took any notice.

In fact, it wasn't until her heir, as King Edward VII, took over his own Royal Train that the drivers were given the instruction to 'go as fast as you like.' In later trains, Queen Victoria had an electric bell installed in her coach to summon members of her entourage. It was unique in that once pressed, the bell remained ringing until it was answered, so nobody could pretend that they hadn't heard it.

That first train journey by what could be described as 'The Royal Train' was so successful that Victoria decided she would return to Windsor by the same method ten days later, even considering rail travel so safe that she took the infant Prince of Wales, later King Edward VII, with her. Her Majesty would end up having no fewer than 16 Royal Trains at her disposal, more than any subsequent monarch.

Prince Albert was so delighted at his wife's acceptance of rail travel following her first experience that he began to involve himself in ways to improve the Royal carriages. The suspension on that first train was very basic with just four wheels to each carriage, so comfort was not as it later became. There were no 'facilities' on board and it was Albert who, eight years after that first trip, suggested to the GWR that a lavatory should be installed in the Royal Train. The company agreed, and in 1850 the first lavatory in a train anywhere in the world, was introduced. Prince Albert, as with Prince Philip, 100 years later, was intensely fascinated by all things practical and he made many suggestions about improvements to the train, as he did with the Royal Yacht *Victoria and*

BELOW: *Two views of Queen Victoria's saloons. The interior of Her Majesty's Day Sitting Room, with its heavy, over-furnished style of the time, is in marked contrast to the simplicity of later Royal saloons. The exterior of the coaches was painted in (LNWR) Plum & Spilt Milk as this was long before the purple colour known as 'Royal Claret' was introduced. (Patrick Kingston Collection)*

Albert when that came into service, just as Prince Philip did with *Britannia*.

Just 18 months after that first rail journey the directors of the London & Birmingham Railway, anticipating the benefits of Royal patronage during a projected visit to the Midland counties, built a Royal saloon for Her Majesty's pleasure.

It was 15ft long by 7ft wide and was described in the *Lincoln Mercury* newspaper as being 'fitted up as a drawing room, combining convenience and ease. By the ingenious arrangement of an elegant curtain in the centre of the saloon, a division is made by which two distinct apartments can be formed.

'To obviate the inconvenience of passing through tunnels in darkness, a grand glass lamp is inserted at each end of the carriage, both of which are under the control of a guard, who will turn on the light as the train enters the tunnel. The temperature of the carriage is governed by a ventilator inserted into the centre of the

roof which can be opened or shut at pleasure, and a proper degree of heat is kept up by means of hot-water pipes which can circulate in every direction under the carriage.

'The exterior is surmounted by a magnificent regal crown, carved and elaborately gilded, which has the effect of imparting a most finished appearance to the design.'

The same edition of the newspaper included a brief report on the actual journey which took place on 27 November 1843.

'The interior of the Royal carriage is furnished with exotica and includes a handsome ottoman on which the Queen sat. On this occasion she was dressed in a satin plaid dress with a black velvet tunic and an open straw bonnet trimmed with blue. Prince Albert was attired in a blue surtout coat, with tweed trousers.

'… The special train appointed to convey Her Majesty and Prince Albert consisted of five first-class carriages, the Royal saloon carriage and three trucks. The train arrived thirty minutes early at five minutes to eleven o'clock … then proceeded to Wolverton at 12.30pm where the Queen was to partake of lunch, and the journey was completed in one hour and ten minutes, a journey of 35 miles.'

It was the acquisition of three private Royal residences in Scotland, Norfolk and on the Isle of Wight, which caused rail travel to be brought into the national consciousness. Once Queen Victoria had agreed to use trains to travel between London and her homes in Balmoral, Sandringham and Osborne House, the railway companies rushed to complete lines between these areas and London, and consequently the travelling public benefited.

Publicity-conscious railway companies were always seeking new ways to attract attention to their coaches and shamelessly exploited their connections with Royalty, no matter how slight.

Queen Victoria made her first trip from Scotland to England on 28 September 1848, although the journey had not been planned originally. She had intended to sail on the Royal Yacht from Aberdeen but when the captain saw the weather forecast he realised he would be unable to leave harbour with his Royal passengers. The only

LEFT: *The lavish interior of a Royal coach during the reign of Queen Victoria, with its stylish and unique ceiling, beautiful curtains and armchairs and sofa – which were not, apparently, as comfortable as they looked. (Patrick Kingston Collection)*

alternatives were to travel by coach, which would have taken many days, or rail which again would have involved at least a couple of days travel. The Queen decided she would use the train and, as there were no Royal saloons for Her Majesty's exclusive use, (Scottish railway companies had not at that time started to build their own Royal carriages) she travelled from Aberdeen to Perth on the first leg back to Windsor in a first-class carriage of the Aberdeen Railway. It was another 'first' for Victoria as it was the first time a British sovereign had ridden in an 'ordinary' train.

In those far off days, trains did not run non-stop for such long distances, so the Royal journey took over two days and involved overnight stays – at Perth and Crewe – before Her Majesty completed her journey at Euston station in London before finishing, as usual, with a

ABOVE: *The drawing room/day compartment of Queen Victoria's LNWR saloon. Note the quilted ceiling and delicate tapestry furnishings and the coverings to the oil lamps. Although by now, 1895, electric lighting had been installed, Her Majesty was not impressed, preferring the softer glow of the oil lamps.*
(Patrick Kingston Collection)

carriage drive to Buckingham Palace.

However, Victoria later said she thoroughly enjoyed the experience of her first long distance train ride and was not in the least impatient at the disruption of her plans, even though her Household – and the railway employees – nearly 'had kittens' making the necessary emergency arrangements.

The journey between London and the Highlands of Scotland was to become one of the most frequent Victoria would make in her long reign. Balmoral Castle (it was known merely as Balmoral House when Prince Albert first acquired it), was a favourite holiday home for the Queen and her family and once the railway lines and trains had become established, she refused to travel any other way. It was on 17 October 1866 that the final stretch of the line from Aberdeen to Ballater, via Banchory and Aboyne, was opened.

On Friday, 27 August 1880, the Court Circular revealed that Queen Victoria and Princess Beatrice travelled from Osborne House on the Isle of Wight and then joined the Royal Train to journey up to Balmoral. The train took them as far as Ballater, a journey of some 627 miles, with several 'comfort' stops in between.

It was also during the 1880s that Victoria spent some

£5,000 of her own money (approximately £356,959 today) on a return journey from London to Ballater. Look-out men were stationed every 200 yards of the entire length of the track, meaning 4,500 men were needed to line the route. Even for Her Majesty this was a considerable sum when she spent on average around £10,000 a year on all her rail travel.

In 1886, the Royal Waiting Room at Ballater was built to a design approved by Queen Victoria and the platforms were extended so that the Royal Guard of Honour could be paraded whenever Her Majesty arrived at Ballater station. Appropriately, exactly one hundred years later, Victoria's great-great-great-granddaughter, Elizabeth II, visited the Royal Waiting Room and she also inspected a Royal Guard of Honour on the platform.

During the reign of Queen Victoria the practice of the Prime Minister of the time attending Her Majesty for a few days in the summer holidays began, and it has continued to this day. Until the Second World War, the journey was invariably undertaken by rail and many Government ministers, and visiting foreign Royalty – expressed their opinions that the rural line between Aberdeen and Ballater offered some of the most beautiful scenic views in the country – if not in the world.

The Tsar of Russia said he had not realised that Britain was a country so rich in magnificent beauty. He also praised the efficiency of the railway system, comparing it favourably with that in his home country.

As has been stated, Queen Victoria believed it was unsafe to eat on the move and insanitary to bathe or use the lavatory, which is why there were so many small halts on the route between England and Scotland, all fully equipped with what passed in those days as luxury facilities. The Queen would order the train to stop wherever and whenever she felt like it; timetables meant nothing to her, or, to be fair, to the railway companies vying for the honour of conveying their Royal passenger.

Everyone, including rail barons, accommodated Queen Victoria. Breakfast was Her Majesty's favourite meal, but she ate at a fast pace, so, just as today at state banquets, when the Duke of Edinburgh has finished, everyone's plate is removed, finished or not, the Household had to eat in a hurry because when the

Queen had eaten enough, they had to leave, frequently when they were only halfway through their meal.

Every rail company in Britain was quick to realise that Royal patronage would not only provide excellent public relations, but could also be used for commercial advantage. Just as today, a Royal Warrant is considered to be a stamp of approval with many people believing that if it's good enough for Royalty it is good enough for them. As soon as Queen Victoria and her family began using railways, the public flocked to become passengers.

Advances in railway design were rapid as the popularity of this new form of transport took hold and the Royal carriages were in the vanguard of this new technology. The London & North Western Railway was able to boast that they were the first to produce a Royal Train where it was possible to move from one carriage to another. They did this by building a short gangway between Queen Victoria's day saloon and her night carriage. However, they were unable to persuade Her Majesty to try the new system; she still insisted on having the train stopped whenever she wanted to move from one saloon to the next. Later in her reign, when electric lighting was introduced on trains for the first time, she refused to allow it to be switched on in her carriage, preferring to stick to candles and oil lamps.

The Great Western Railway considered itself to be the instigator of Royal travel, having carried Queen Victoria on that first journey, and it was determined that it would also be the first to build a line specially for the Queen. So it was that on 8 October 1849, less than 18 months after that first trip, that the GWR opened the branch line from Slough to Windsor with a station only a few hundred yards away from the Henry VIII Gate at the castle. Victoria had apparently overcome her earlier objections to having a station so near her home, in order to be able to enjoy the convenience of being able to catch a train without having to travel by road all the way to Slough.

BELOW: *Queen Victoria's 12-wheel saloon of the London & North Western Railway (LNWR). Originally built at the company's Wolverton Works in 1869 as twin saloons connected by a flexible gangway, they were joined together in 1895. The Queen had refused to walk from one saloon to the other unless the train was stationary. The Queen made her last journey in this saloon from Ballater, the station for Balmoral, to Windsor in November 1900. (Patrick Kingston Collection)*

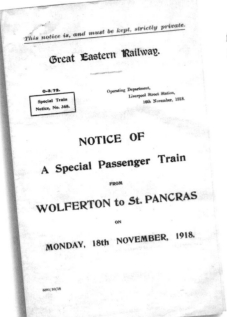

Great Eastern Railway.

0-3/72.

Special Train
Notice. No. 368.

Operating Department,
Liverpool Street Station,
16th November, 1918.

NOTICE OF

A Special Passenger Train

FROM

WOLFERTON to St. PANCRAS

ON

MONDAY, 18th NOVEMBER, 1918.

5281/10/18

from Paddington to Dartmouth in Devon non-stop. It was the first time any train had achieved this. Scheduled services completed the journey in 5 hours 45 minutes; the Royal Train did it in 4 hours. To enable this record run to be accomplished, new water troughs over a mile long were laid by the GWR between Durston and Taunton. Without this it would not have been possible to run the train without stopping to take on water.

Edward VII did not care for Balmoral as much as his mother had and usually only travelled there once a year. However, this was enough for the Great North of Scotland Railway to construct its own Royal Train in 1902, which comprised six special coaches. This Royal Train was used only between Aberdeen and Ballater, apart from one occasion when it was 'borrowed' by the Great Northern Railway to convey The King south of the Scottish border. It was used for a small number of journeys in England before finally leaving Ollerton (the home of Lord and Lady Saville, The King's hosts), to return to Ballater.

Sandringham remained Edward VII's favourite home, both for the shooting and because it was comparatively easy to get to from London, and the tiny Wolferton station was busier then than probably at any other time.

Queen Alexandra was involved in one of the most potentially embarrassing episodes on the Royal Train in 1909 during an evening meal. The senior footman who was serving her accidentally dislodged her hairpiece (worn to conceal baldness) and apologised profusely.

Her Majesty saw the funny side and laughed off the incident, so too did The King, much to the relief of the steward and everyone else on board.

The line between Wolferton and London was used continuously by Edward and Alexandra until he died in 1910. His heir, King George V, continued to travel back and forth on the Royal Train saying: 'At Sandringham I have a home; in London I have only a house,' a reference to Buckingham Palace which he disliked.

The year 1913 saw George V and Queen Mary use the Royal Train for an entire week, arguably the longest period it has ever been in use continuously. They made many stops and did not always sleep on board, often staying overnight with friends and it was no doubt the first and possibly only time the Royal Train has been fully utilised as a 'mobile home'.

George V always travelled to Sandringham on the Royal Train for the Christmas holidays, but 1935 saw his last journey by rail as a reigning monarch. His Majesty sadly died on 20 January 1936 and his coffin was brought back to London in the hearse coach that had been used in 1925 to convey the body of his mother, Queen Alexandra. A ten-coach funeral train was assembled with all windows blacked out as they travelled from Wolferton to King's Lynn and thence on to King's Cross.

Generations of the Royal Family used the rail service, including The Queen, The Queen Mother and Princess Margaret and they particularly enjoyed the Christmas journey when they used to travel from London for the holiday. When King George VI died at Sandringham in February 1952, his body was brought back to London on the Royal Train.

Sadly, as with so many other historic stations and lines, Wolferton and the line connecting it to London, closed in 1966. It was the end of a magical era in Royal rail travel that had lasted just over 100 years and had seen more changes than even the most imaginative of Victorian passengers could have envisaged.

RIGHT: *Wolferton station, with ex-LNER Class D16 4-4-0 No. 62614 waiting to convey the Royal Family back to King's Cross in January 1951 after they had spent Christmas at Sandringham. (Alan Howard, Patrick Kingston Collection)*

CHAPTER 7

Royal funeral trains

$\mathcal{I}$F THERE is one occasion more than any other when everything has to go according to plan, even more than with the usual Household attention to detail, it is when a Royal Train is carrying the body of a member of the Royal Family to its final resting place. British Royalty has retained the knack of burying its dead with enormous ceremonial style, and the Royal Train has made a significant contribution to maintaining this enviable reputation.

The timing of the last journey has to be absolutely accurate because it involves so many other organisations, and the various aspects of a sad and dignified occasion have to be observed without losing any of the efficiency that is expected of Royal events.

As with everything else to do with Royalty, nothing is left until the last minute. Preparations for Royal funeral trains begin several years before they are expected to be needed, and are then updated on an annual basis as requirements change, people die or their status alters.

RIGHT: *The funeral train of King George VI steams away from Paddington station for Windsor, hauled by No. 4082* **Windsor Castle***, 15 February 1952. (Patrick Kingston Collection)*

Precedent is everything in preparing for a Royal duty and often, as macabre as it may sound, the principals involved will concern themselves with the most tiny detail of their own funeral.

Such was the case in 1973, when Earl Mountbatten of Burma began preparing for his funeral. He told the present author that he thoroughly enjoyed making the arrangements and was only sorry that he would not be there to see them brought to fruition. He even selected the menu for the meal to be eaten during the journey.

As it happened, Lord Mountbatten died much more suddenly than even he could have imagined when he, together with several members of his family and a young Irish boy, were blown up by an IRA bomb planted on his fishing boat at Mullaghmore in Southern Ireland, in August 1979. But the arrangements he had made more than five years earlier were followed to the letter.

Funeral trains were, and still are, referred to as 'special trains' in all correspondence and the following letter from the Royal Train authority to the Lord Chamberlain's Office illustrates the meticulous planning that precedes any and every Royal occasion, even when, as is the case here, the actual date the train will be required is unknown at that time.

LEFT: *The scene on Platform 11 at Waterloo station as the coffin of the late Earl Mountbatten of Burma is carried towards the special funeral train, watched by members of his family, for the journey to Romsey, Hampshire. The Queen and other members of the Royal Family also travelled on the train, which consisted of ordinary first class coaches in the then-British Rail colours of blue and light grey which, for security reasons, was less obvious than the Royal Train. The coffin travelled in a specially-adapted luggage van, known to railway staff as a BG, bearing the running number M80867. (Patrick Kingston)*

R. J. Hill Esq. M.V.O., M.B.E.
Secretary Lord Chamberlain's Office
St James's Palace
London SW1

4th April 1974

D.339 ST

Referring to your letter of 12 July 1973 and our recent discussion in connection with a special train from Waterloo to Romsey and return on an unspecified train from Waterloo to Romsey and return on an unspecified date in the future, arrangements could be made on the following lines and perhaps you will kindly let me know in due course if they are acceptable.

```
                    TRAIN TIMINGS
        Waterloo (Platform 11)        - dep 1255
        Romsey                        - arr 1430
        Romsey                        - dep 1710
        Waterloo (Platform 11)        - arr 1842

           TRAIN FORMATION (departing Waterloo)
Locomotive
First-Class Coach (Open seating type)
First-Class Coach (Open seating type) - For approx. 70 V.I.P.'s
Restaurant Car
First-Class Coach (Compartment seating) - For 10 principals.
First-Class Coach (Open seating type)  - Lord Chamberlain's party
                                         Railway Officers
                                         and Police
H.M. Forces personnel (Total approx. 30).
Brake vehicle - 36 seats available if required (including 12 1st class)
Van - Appropriately fitted.

    The formation on the return journey will be the same, except that
    the van will be detached and left at Romsey.

                    REFRESHMENTS
Luncheon can be provided on the forward journey and two suggested menus
are listed below for you to make a choice. When considering suitable
menus, account has to be taken of the limited time available to service
approximately 100 luncheons from one restaurant car.
        (A)                         (B)
        Melon                       Fruit Juices
        Cold Scotch Salmon          Cold Chicken & Ham
        Mayonnaise Sauce            Green Salad
        Green & Potato Salad        New Potatoes
        Boiled Potatoes
        Cheese Board                Fruit Salad and Cream
        Coffee                      Coffee
```

So far as wines are concerned on both the forward and return journeys,
I feel that the selection should be left to you and perhaps you will
let me know your preference when advising choice of menu. The normal
spirits etc. will, of course be available. Teas and light refreshments
will also be available on the return journey.

    If you should require clarification on any point, please do not
    hesitate to contact me.

Within days of the death of Lord Mountbatten, every detail had been finalised and approved and the following document was issued to all those who needed to be informed.

BRITISH RAIL – SOUTHERN REGION

PRIVATE – FOR THE INFORMATION – Chief Operating Manager
OF THE STAFF CONCERNED ONLY – WATERLOO

September 1979 **FUNERAL OF LORD MOUNTBATTEN**
1255 ROYAL TRAIN WATERLOO TO ROMSEY, 5.9.79

Passengers and officials will travel in the train as follows –

Locomotives	Driver W. H. Turner
	Driver's Assistant B. Clarke
	Motive Power Inspector G. Reynolds
	Fitter A. Pascoe
Escort Vehicle M2906	S. Butler
	E. Benson – Royal Train Staff
	Police Officers
Open First (lettered A) 53066	21 people – see attached list
Open First 53070	31 people – see attached list
Restaurant Buffet W1652 (kitchen trailing)	A. J. Simpson, Head of Operations, Travellers' Fare
	A. G. Whitbread, Group Train Catering Manager
	Travellers' Fare Staff

Corridor First
M13550
– centre non smoking compartment (not tabled)	The Queen – The Duke of Edinburgh
	The Prince of Wales
– adjacent non smoking compartment (long table fitted)	The Princess Anne, Mrs Mark Phillips
	Captain Mark Phillips
– other compartments – 11 people (tabled)	The family of Lord Mountbatten

N.B. The Queen will enter and leave by the trailing doors.

Open First (lettered C) S3065   31 people – see attached list

Corridor Composite –
Brake
(S21273)
(Van trailing)
- 1 x 2nd compartment – Police Officers
- 1 x 2nd compartment
- 1 x 2nd compartment
- 1 x 1st compartment - Mr Jewell
- 1 x 1st compartment – J. Palette

M. C. Holmes

C. M. S. Maguire

J. E. Vine

Divisional Inspector R. Russell

A. C. Waller

Guard's compartment –
Brake Van (M80867)
(large compartment
leading)

Guard W. Simpson

Mr M. Kenyon

Fleet Chief Petty Officer

Details of motorcar processions are attached hereto
M. C. Holmes – CHIEF OPERATING MANAGER

A COACH

Prince and Princess Georg of Hanover
Prince Andrew of Hohenlohe-Langenburg
Mrs Robert Van Eyck
Monsieur and Madame Derien
Princess Frederika of Hanover
Lieutenant-Colonel and Mrs Harold Phillips
Major and Mrs David Butter
Prince and Princess Andrew Romanoff of Russia
Prince Dimitri of Russia
Mr and Mrs Reginald Eastwood
Mr Peter Eastwood
Lady Iris Mountbatten
The Duke and Duchess of Abercorn
Mrs Vihaya Lakshmi Pandit

THE QUEEN'S COACH

The Queen
The Duke of Edinburgh
The Prince of Wales
The Princess Anne, Mrs Mark Phillips
Captain Mark Phillips

Hon. Norton Knatchbull	Mr David and Lady Pamela Hicks
Hon. Michael John Knatchbull	Miss Edwina Hicks
Hon. Joanna Knatchbull	Mr Ashley Hicks
Hon. Amanda Knatchbull	Miss India Hicks
Hon. Phillip Knatchbull	
	Miss Penelope Eastwood

C COACH

The Duke and Duchess of Gloucester
The Duke and Duchess of Kent
Prince and Princess Michael of Kent
Princess Alexandra and the Hon. Angus Ogilvy
Sir Philip Moore
Lord Rupert Nevill
Lieutenant-Commander Robert Guy
King of Norway
King Constantine and Queen Anne-Marie of the Hellenes
King and Queen of Sweden
Grand Duke and Grand Duchess of Luxembourg
Count of Barcelona
Prince Albert of Liege
Prince Georg of Denmark
The Earl of Malmesbury
Mr John Barratt
2 Protection Officers – 6 Duty

LORD MOUNTBATTEN'S FUNERAL TRAIN TO ROMSEY

	Duty Coach		Duty Coach
Lord Chamberlain	C	Major Chamberlayne-Macdonald	C
Sir Eric Penn	C	Sir Ronald Brockman	B
Colonel Johnston	B	Major Shane Blewitt	B
Sir John Miller	B	Captain Macfarlane	B
Mr. John Titman	B	Mr M. Kenyon	C
Mr Jewell	C	Fleet Chief Petty Officer,	
Dr Southward	C	London Bearer Party	C
		Sergeant Evans	B
			Total 14

RIGHT: *Newlyweds Prince Charles and Princess Diana board the Royal Train at Waterloo as they set off on their honeymoon in July 1981. In 1997, after the funeral of Diana, Princess of Wales, the Royal Train was used to carry the chief mourners to Althorp where she was to be interred. (Getty Images)*

Eighteen years later, the Royal Household and the operators of the Royal Train were to experience an occasion which had no precedent and for which the organisation had to be arranged in extreme haste. It was the train carrying the chief mourners who had attended the funeral of Diana, Princess of Wales, from London Euston to Long Buckby in Northamptonshire in order that she could be interred at the Spencer family home at Althorp, following her tragic and unexpected death in Paris on 31 August 1997. Nevertheless, in spite of the lack of warning, everything went according to a quickly arranged plan and the rail journey was executed with precision and the sort of respectful efficiency one would expect.

Diana's body had already been taken by road from Westminster Abbey to Althorp, with large crowds lining the route throughout.

Following the funeral service on Saturday, 6 September 1997, the Royal Train left Euston at 12.30, arriving at Long Buckby at 14.05.

There were five coaches including No 2921 Escort vehicle containing Chris Hillyard the Royal Train Foreman and members of his staff, plus several British Transport Police Officers and the late Norman Pattenden MBE, at that time the Royal Train Officer. Next to them were the two Royal Household saloons Nos 2918 and 2919 and the Household dining saloon No 2917. Making up the train was the power car No 2920.

The locomotives were No 47798 *Prince William*, which led the train and on the rear was No 47799 *Prince Henry*.

His Royal Highness The Prince of Wales was accompanied by his sons, Prince William and Prince Harry and also in the party were members of Diana's family: The Hon. Mrs Shand-Kydd (Diana's mother), Earl Spencer (her brother), Lady Sarah McCorquodale (sister) and her husband with their two children, Emily and George. Sir (now Lord) Robert Fellowes (The Queen's private secretary and brother-in-law of Diana) with his wife Lady Jane Fellowes (Diana's sister) and their three children, Laura, Alexander and Eleanor.

In another carriage there were additional passengers including Miss Josie Borain, Rev. Victor Malan, Paul Burrell (Diana's butler), Colin Tebbutt (Royalty Protection Department) and two RPG officers.

The timings of this final journey of the late Diana, Princess of Wales were as accurate as any carried out by the Royal Train. It left its base at Wolverton Centre Sidings at 07.56 precisely, two minutes early, arriving at Euston No 18 platform, seven minutes late (due to a signal delay outside Euston awaiting completion of BTP searches), at 09.22, three hours before it was due to depart. A 'screen' train of Class 325 electric multiple units had been placed on No 16 platform at the request of British Transport Police.

The conclusion of the funeral service at Westminster Abbey was marked by a one-minute silence and railway staff on Platform 18 were invited to observe the silence in front of escort car No 2921. The public address system between Platforms 15 and 18 was then switched off to avoid intrusion.

In order to maintain privacy for the funeral party, only the Train Officer, Norman Pattenden, and the

Train Foreman, Chris Hillyard, were present on the platform when the motorcade arrived at 12.25. All other staff took up their positions within the train until departure time, which was 12.31 – one minute late. The slight delay was because the locomotives were not started up until the Principals had entrained due to the sensitivity of the occasion. Normally, they would have already been started up by the time the Royal party had joined the train.

A very cautious departure was made from Euston until the rear of the train was fully on the Down Slow Line, the movements of the party on board being an unknown quantity. Nevertheless, the one-minute late start was recovered on the 32mph timing to Willesden West London Junction, which was passed on time at 12.42. As far as Bletchley, the journey called for a realistic average speed of 62mph. The Train Officer instructed the driver to reduce speed to 45mph through Bletchley South Junction in order to maintain ride comfort in that area. North of Bletchley, the timings gave speeds of 47mph to Milton Keynes Central, 51mph to Hanslope Junction and 49mph to Northampton. Yet even on this unique Royal Train, consideration was given to other rail users and the time allowed between Northampton and Long Buckby was reduced by three minutes so as to minimise delay to the 12.54 Euston–Birmingham New St. service.

The required speed from Northampton to Long Buckby was 41mph and Traction Inspector Mark Winkworth and Driver Frosdick of Willesden, brought the train to a correctly positioned stand at 14.04.51 – some nine seconds early.

After arrival at Long Buckby

at 14.05, it remained for only eight minutes for the passengers to detrain before leaving again at 14.13. Nuneaton was the next stop for a driver change at 14.40, leaving at 15.00 finally arriving back at the Wolverton depot at 16.09, the exact time for which it had been scheduled.

For the Royal Train crew it had been the saddest experience, as they had carried the Princess – with the Prince of Wales – many times during the first year of their marriage in 1981 (see Chapter 3, 'The Train today').

LEFT: *Wherever she went the Princess drew large crowds. (Mick Foster)*

SATURDAY, 6 SEPTEMBER 1997

LONDON (EUSTON) TO LONG BUCKBY

Euston	Depart	12 30
Watford Junction	Pass	12 57
Tring	Pass	13 11
Milton Keynes Central	Pass	13 32
Northampton	Pass	13 51
Long Buckby	Arrive	14 05

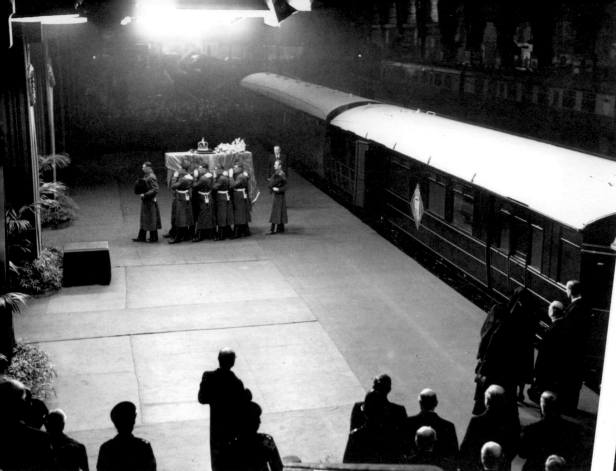

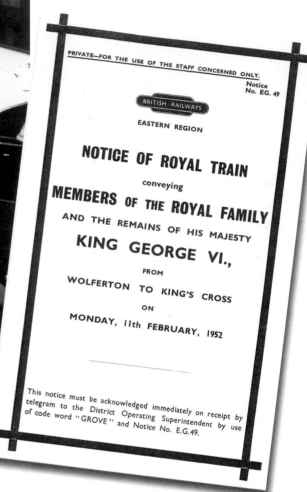

ABOVE: *King George VI's coffin, surmounted by his crown, is carried from the Royal Train at King's Cross station on 11 February 1952, after arriving from Sandringham, where His Majesty had died five days earlier. (Getty Images)*

FACING PAGE: *King George VI's funeral train leaving Paddington for Windsor seemingly hauled by No. 4082* **Windsor Castle***, 15 February 1952. The locomotive was actually No. 7013* **Bristol Castle** *with name and number plates exchanged, as No. 4082 was under repair. (Patrick Kingston Collection)*

King George VI died in February 1952 at Sandringham and his body was brought back to London for the Lying-in-State at Westminster Abbey before the interment at Windsor Castle.

As His Majesty had been in poor health for some years, his death while sudden, did not leave the authorities completely unprepared. The Eastern Region of British Railways was charged with bringing the 'Special Passenger Train' from King's Lynn to Wolferton to collect the coffin and then carry it to King's Cross station. The arrangements were immaculate and among the special instructions issued to all staff prior to the journey was the following:

'All shunting at stations and yards en route must be stopped whilst the Royal Train is passing. All trains passing the Royal Special must reduce speed to 15 miles per hour whilst doing so. As far as possible the public must be excluded from the stations en route, and every effort must be made to secure quietness whilst the Royal Train is passing.'

Further notes to the operating staff included information about the stopping point at King's Cross where the 'Grove' train (the Royal Train codeword,

ABOVE: *Royal Train notice, King George VI.*

adopted during the Second World War), must be brought to a stop with the centre of the leading engine cab opposite a point where a hand signalman will be stationed to indicate the correct place. The instructions continued 'At both Wolferton and King's Cross, once the train engine has been coupled to the train and the brake tested by the guard, the automatic brake must be entirely destroyed and the brake held on the train until the driver receives instructions from the stationmaster or the officer in charge of the train to re-create the brake.'

No scheduled trains were permitted to interrupt the running of the funeral train, with services such as the 9.11pm South Lynn to King's Cross ordered to be kept clear at King's Lynn; the 10.12am Cambridge to King's Lynn (via March) had to be held at Magdalen Road. Seven other services were ordered to be held clear of King's Lynn and the timings between Wolferton and King's Cross (No 1 platform) were detailed at no fewer than 38 points on the route. The funeral train left Wolferton at 12.05pm precisely and arrived at King's Cross on time at 2.45pm. In spite of the instruction to exclude the public from the stations through which the Royal Train would pass, thousands of people stood in respectful silence at many points along the route.

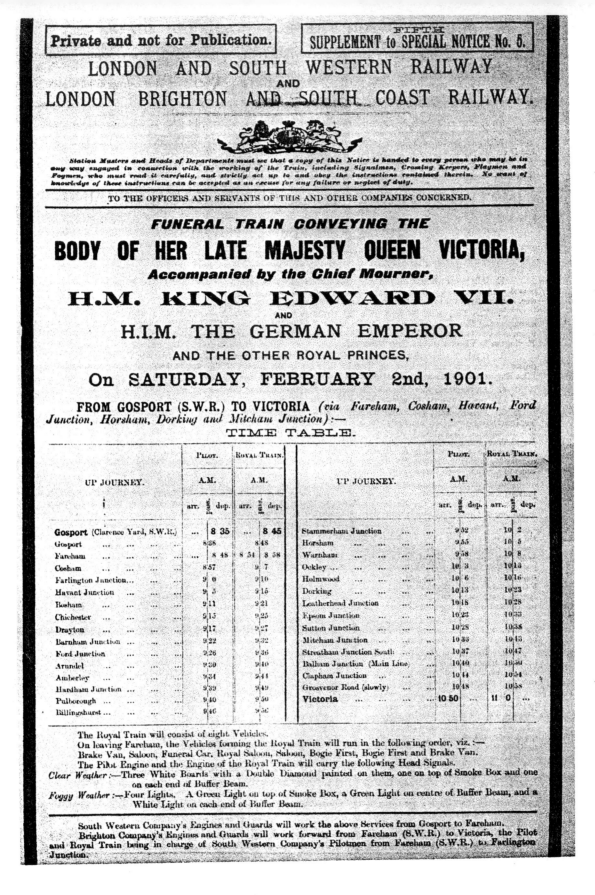

LEFT: *Notice of the Royal Funeral Train bearing the late Queen Victoria. It was claimed that more crowned heads were present for her funeral than at any other occasion. Her heir, the new King Edward VII, led the mourners, accompanied by His Imperial Majesty, the German Emperor.*

RIGHT: *The funeral train for Queen Victoria, seen at Platform B of Paddington Station, 2 February 1901. It was headed by 'Atbara' class 4-4-0, No. 3373, named* **Royal Sovereign** *for the occasion. (Getty Images)*

The death of Queen Victoria prefaced one of the most remarkable funeral train journeys ever. Steam locomotives from three different railway companies powered the trains that carried her body from the South Coast to Victoria station in London and then from Paddington to Windsor, before interment at the Frogmore Mausoleum in the grounds of Windsor Castle. Her Majesty had decreed that there should be no public Lying-in-State and only a semi-private ceremony was held at Osborne House before she was carried to the mainland.

There have been many accounts of the funeral trains of Queen Victoria, almost all varying in detail and

accuracy. Possibly the most comprehensive is that written by Norman Pattenden, former Royal Train Officer for many years and the man most closely associated with Royal travel by rail until his death. Mr Pattenden researched the files of all the railway companies involved in the funeral transport arrangements of Queen Victoria and his report of Her Majesty's last LSWR journey is a model of descriptive detail:

Queen Victoria died early in the evening of Tuesday, 22nd January 1901 at Osborne House on the Isle of Wight. Arrangements for her funeral had been made many years before and

LEFT: *This interior view of the Royal hearse carriage, in which Her Majesty's coffin was conveyed, shows the pomp accorded to her final journey. (Patrick Kingston Collection)*

amended practically every year. Although contingency plans were in place should the death occur on the Isle of Wight, it had generally been expected that funeral transport would be needed from Windsor not Osborne.

On Friday, 1st February the Royal Yacht Alberta *(smallest of the Royal Yachts) carried the body of the Queen across the Solent to Portsmouth from where it would be taken by Royal Train to London before the funeral service which was to be held the following day, 2nd February in St George's Chapel, Windsor Castle. The Queen's successor, her eldest son, King Edward VII, had decreed that there should be a carriage funeral procession through the streets of London, so that the people could show their respects, before the final stage of the journey by GWR (appropriately the railway company with whom she had made her first railway journey in 1842) from Paddington to Windsor, where she was to rest alongside her late husband, Prince Albert.*

The first part of the journey, from Royal Clarence Yard, Gosport (Her Majesty's personal station) to Fareham, was assigned to LSWR (London & South Western Railway) where it handed over to the LBSCR (London, Brighton & South Coast Railway) Royal Train, for the journey to London Victoria on the personal instructions of the King, in spite of the fact that Queen Victoria was known to have a long-standing dislike of the company, or indeed anything to do with Brighton since an over enthusiastic crowd had annoyed her in the 1840s. However, the vehicles chosen by LBSCR had been built only as recently as 1898 for the King when he was Prince of Wales and he felt they were far more appropriate than the old-fashioned coaches of the LNWR and even the GWR. But it was a GWR coach that was used to carry the late Queen's body on her final journey. It was No 229, a saloon that had been altered for the Diamond Jubilee in 1897, and furnished appropriately as a hearse coach being lined with white satin and purple hangings.

The train consisted of eight carriages in all, needed because of the large numbers of mourners who accompanied the coffin, most of them members of European Royalty, and practically all related in some way to Queen Victoria.

Although the railway officials had planned in advance the composition of the train, there was still a great deal of confusion as mourners of different rank tried to find their allotted places onboard the Royal Train. The only mourner who apparently had no difficulty in finding his correct place was the senior Royal on board, His Imperial Majesty, The Emperor of Germany, who was to accompany his mother-in-law's body to London.

Added to the fact that the train was too long for the platform at Gosport, which in the past had been used only for the 'short train' of Queen Victoria, and there was no corridor connecting the different coaches, and the train had to be in reverse order, there was a distinctly icy atmosphere between the two railway companies, LSWR and LBSCR, who each blamed the other for the fiasco, and would continue to do so for many years.

As it was, the start of the journey from Gosport was delayed by eight minutes – unheard of for Royal Trains – and things got worse as the day wore on. Another ten minutes were lost at Fareham, which meant they were in danger of not arriving on time at Victoria where the new King, Edward VII, was waiting impatiently to meet the train. Everyone knew how much His Majesty hated unpunctuality, so the order was given to the driver to go as fast as he could. He actually achieved speeds of over 80mph,

something Queen Victoria would never have allowed in her lifetime, and managed not only to make up the lost time, but to arrive at Victoria station two minutes early.

Queen Victoria's Royal standard bedecked coffin was carried in a gun-carriage procession through the silent streets from Victoria station to Paddington, from where she would be taken back to Windsor.

The GWR was perfectly prepared for the occasion. Paddington station was draped in purple and two special trains were despatched before the departure of the Royal Train taking the invited guests of non-Royal rank: Cabinet ministers, foreign ambassadors and others of diplomatic rank. GWR notes of the time indicated that tickets would not be issued for this journey but that the invitations should be shown as proof that the holder was permitted to travel.

By the time the funeral cortege had reached Paddington, the GWR funeral hearse coach had been detached from the LBSCR train that had brought it from Gosport and Fareham, and inserted into the GWR Royal funeral train on Platform 8. The engine that was to pull the train, Athara, had even been renamed Royal Sovereign for the occasion, with its headlamp covered in purple cloth, a white disc over each buffer with the Royal coat-of-arms prominently displayed on each side of the locomotive, also draped in purple.

The Royal Train left Paddington at 1.40 in the afternoon and GWR employees who had been instructed to stand along the line at intervals marked the entire route to Windsor. They had been there for some hours in freezing temperatures and as the train passed, each man doffed his cap and bowed his head. It was a touching scene that was never to be repeated.'

The funeral train of Victoria's successor, King Edward VII, saw the arrival in Britain by sea of so many foreign Royalty, Heads of State and other distinguished guests, that the South Eastern & Chatham Railway was forced to mount no fewer than ten special trains to convey them from Dover, Folkestone and Port Victoria to London Victoria on Wednesday, 18 May 1910 and Thursday, 19 May 1910.

The first train, carrying HRH The Duke d'Costa, left Folkestone at 1.15pm promptly, arriving at Platform 9, Victoria station at 3.10pm. This was followed by special train No 2 from Dover with five Royals on board: TRH The Crown Prince of Roumania, Prince Maximilian of Baden, The Grand Duke of Hesse, Prince Philip and Prince Leopold of Saxe-Coburg, who departed at 3 o'clock and arrived at 4.25pm. Only ten minutes separated this train from the next, that of HM The King of Portugal and HRH The Crown Prince of Servia, leaving Prince of Wales Pier at 3.10pm arriving at Victoria at 5 o'clock. After another 20 minutes, the President of France, Monsieur Pichon, accompanied by the Chinese Mission and the Turkish Mission, departed from Dover's Admiralty Pier. Prince Henry of The Netherlands came next in special train No 5 departing from Port Victoria at 5.15pm followed by The King of The Belgians and Prince Rupert of Bavaria. By now the trains were running thick

ABOVE: *A posed view, for the official GWR photographer, of the funeral train for King Edward VII which ran from Paddington to Windsor on 20 May 1910, drawn by No. 4021* **King Edward***; the hearse carriage is the fourth from the locomotive. (Patrick Kingston Collection)*

being expected. 'Reliable men to be placed at facing points over which the Royal Train will run, some 30 minutes before it is due and remain there until it has passed. All approach road gates are to be closed and locked 30 minutes before the Royal Train is due. The fogmen must take up their posts (whether it is foggy or not) 30 minutes before the Royal Train is due. The locomotive department is to arrange an emergency engine to be available at every station in case it is needed. The call sign for the Royal Train is 'R.S.' (Royal Special) to be used by the Emergency Telegraph Instrument. Platelayers to be stationed along the line within signalling distance of each other. All level crossings to be closed with men stationed to prevent anyone accidentally or deliberately obstructing the progress of the Royal Train. Care must be taken to ensure that all passengers on the Royal Train are seated before the signal to start is given. No unauthorized persons are to be allowed on any station through which the Royal Train is passing unless they are passengers travelling in the opposite direction.'

Finally, a note stated that 'No want of knowledge of these instructions can be accepted as an excuse for any failure or neglect of duty.'

King Edward VII had died at Buckingham Palace on 6 May 1910 and after his Lying-in-State in Westminster Hall (when a quarter of a million people passed by the catafalque) his funeral train departed from Paddington station for Windsor where the interment was to take place in St George's Chapel on Friday, 20 May 1910. Eleven coaches made up the train including the same funeral car that had been used for Queen Victoria in 1901, that had been taken out of store for the occasion, and which would prove to be the last time for both passenger and hearse coach. Following this Royal duty the coach was taken to Swindon where it remained until it was broken up in 1912.

For this final journey, the coach carrying the coffin of the late King had been newly carpeted in a delicate shade of lavender and the windows had been blacked out with heavy purple curtains. The walls were also draped in purple and white with subdued lighting used to illuminate the car. At each corner of the Royal standard-bedecked coffin were four circular chairs, also

and fast, with only five minutes between them on occasion. TRH The Grand Duke of Mecklenburg-Strelitz and Prince Charles of Sweden from Dover to Victoria joined Prince Fushima of Japan with three more special trains operating the next day.

The Superintendent of the Line, detailing the exact procedure to be followed, issued 31 separate orders to staff operating the Royal Trains. These included instructions that all goods trains should be shunted out of the way of the line or station through which the Royal Train would pass at least 30 minutes before it was due. No goods, cattle or mineral trains were allowed to travel on adjacent lines within 15 minutes of the Royal Train

upholstered in purple and white and fixed to the floor. During the journey, officers of senior military rank sat with heads bowed 'sitting' guard over their late sovereign.

All the existing Royal saloons were used and a number of ordinary first-class coaches were needed to cope with the large number of Royal mourners. The locomotive was one of the most advanced express engines in the country, named appropriately, *King Edward*, and was draped in sombre purple with the Royal coat-of-arms on either side. The GWR had never before carried so many crowned heads on one train. There were two emperors: the acceding George V and his cousin His Imperial Majesty the German Emperor, Kaiser Wilhelm II, as well as nine reigning monarchs, most of whom were related to Edward VII through their common ancestry with Queen Victoria.

Every station between Paddington and Windsor was closed for the duration of the journey and thousands of people gathered along the line to show their respects to a much-loved monarch.

King George V had led his people through the turbulent years of the First World War when he and his Consort, Queen Mary, had used their Royal Train extensively. So it was appropriate that when His Majesty died, at home in Sandringham, at midnight on 20 January 1936, his body should be brought to London by rail. The King had been in poor health for some time and bulletins were issued daily, and later hourly, regarding his condition.

Two railway companies, the London & North Eastern Railway and the Great Western Railway were to be involved in transporting the coffin. Within hours of His Majesty's death, the LNER had moved the former Royal hearse coach No 46, (last used to carry the remains of his mother, Queen Alexandra in 1925), to their works at Stratford, East London. All the existing furniture was stripped from the coach and a catafalque prepared, with leather straps to secure the coffin when the train was on the move. The windows were blacked out, black velvet carpets were laid and curtains of the same colour and material installed. The walls were lined with black and purple and heavy black drapes covered the doors. The

exterior of the coach was painted in matt black with a white roof, as it had been for Queen Alexandra when her mortal remains were carried from Wolferton to King's Cross on 24 November 1925.

On 23 January, the Royal funeral train was brought to Wolferton, his late Majesty's favourite station, where his body was carried into the hearse car to be returned to London's King's Cross station, via King's Lynn, from where it was hauled by an engine of the Sandringham class, No 2847 *Helmingham Hall*. Officials of the GWR wondered why LNER had not changed the name to *Sandringham* in honour of the King, as the original engine bearing that name, No 2800, was unavailable.

The Royal Funeral Train arrived exactly on time at 2.45pm to be met by a guard of honour which escorted the late King to Westminster Hall where he Lay-in-State for four days.

His Majesty's funeral was to take place in Windsor on Tuesday, 28 January and following the Lying-in-State, a gun-carriage procession, headed by the band of the Household Cavalry, proceeded through the streets of London, past silent crowds, to Paddington station where the Royal funeral train had been relocated from King's Cross. The station was draped in purple and black and a special stand for GWR privileged guests had been erected near Platforms 9 and 10 so they could witness the departure of the Royal Train from Platform 8, the same platform from where the funeral trains of Queen Victoria and King Edward VII had left on their final journeys. Until ten years ago, the concourse alongside Platform 8 at Paddington was used as a taxi rank and the road leading down to it was a gentle slope, ideal for allowing the funeral cortege to descend into the station with dignity and at the correct pace. Today, the gates at the other end of the platform have been closed and taxis now stand near Platform 1.

The GWR was experienced in handling these Royal occasions and they had made several practice runs from Paddington to Windsor in the days when the late King had been Lying-in-State, so that there was little chance of anything going awry. The funeral coaches had been stored at Old Oak Common depot since arriving from Wolferton and even though they belonged to the LNER, the GWR was determined that their section of His

Majesty's final journey by rail, would be remembered as a triumph for the Great Western.

Waiting at Paddington for the arrival of His Majesty's procession were the band of the Coldstream Guards playing suitably funereal music, and before the Royal Train departed with the late King, his widow, Queen Mary, and his successor, King Edward VIII, on board, no fewer than five extra trains were despatched to Windsor carrying all the other Royal, and non-Royal, guests who had been invited to the service in St George's Chapel.

Preparations had been made some years before the death of the King and the steam engine selected to power the funeral train was appropriately named *Windsor Castle*, one His Majesty would, no doubt, have approved of, as he had once ridden on its footplate in 1924 during a visit to Swindon.

The superintendent of the line issued pages of instructions to everyone connected with the journey, and to those employed along the line to Windsor, detailing the precise timings of every section of the 35-minute trip. The orders were followed to the letter and to the haunting lament of *The Flowers of the Forest* played by a lone piper, the Royal Train drew away from Paddington at exactly 12.33pm.

All along the route, thousands of men, women and children, with heads bowed watched from the side of the line and from the bridges under which the train passed, as they paid their final tributes to a greatly respected monarch.

The timetable said the train was due in Windsor at 1.09pm and that was the exact moment when it arrived. His Majesty, who hated unpunctuality at any time, would have been impressed – and the GWR lived up to its formidable reputation.

When arrangements such as these are being made, members of the Royal Family are realists who understand that the practical side of the events need to be made well in advance, even if, as previously stated, some details alter as time goes on.

The Queen knows exactly what is going to happen regarding her own funeral, and so too does the Prince of Wales. There is no sentimentality attached to the death of a sovereign or heir to the throne, as sad as these occasions might be. The business of monarchy has to continue seamlessly and although most ordinary people might find it distressing to discuss their own funeral arrangements, with Royalty the same set of rules can never apply.

CHAPTER 8

Wolverton – home to the Royal Train

T WAS IN 1836 that the London & Birmingham Railway Company decided that the 112-mile distance between the two cities was far too long to expect their rail passengers to travel without being able to stretch their legs and 'relieve themselves'. This being long before that first lavatory on a moving train, and when it came, it was only on the Royal Train initially.

So, with typical Victorian business practice they built a small station and refreshment rooms at the midway point. Thus it was that Wolverton in Buckinghamshire, originally a quiet country village, grew to be one of the most important railway towns in Britain, employing at its height more than 5,000 men and women at the giant railway works that quickly mushroomed around the station.

Robert Stephenson, the founder and builder of the London & Birmingham Railway had decided that not only would Wolverton be the ideal spot to place the station and refreshment rooms, but also the perfect location for his locomotive repair shops. Being just two miles east of

RIGHT: *Arguably the cleanest and neatest railway sheds in the world, Wolverton is the headquarters of the Royal Train, and a showpiece of which those who work there are justifiably proud. Unfortunately, the works are never open to the public. (RAIL magazine)*

ABOVE: *This is where the saloons of the Royal Train carriages are housed and where they are serviced and maintained by a dedicated team of highly skilled engineers, electricians, mechanics and cleaners.* (RAIL magazine)

the old London to Birmingham mail-coach road at Stony Stratford and conveniently positioned for the existing Grand Junction Canal, which could be used to carry all the materials needed to build the works, the infrastructure needed was already in place, so the site was chosen and work began. The confluence of the existing mail-coach road and the canal junction opened up the area for massive investment by the shrewd industrial entrepreneurs of the time.

It took only the comparatively short period of three years for the initial works to be completed in 1839, but in ten years the population of this former quiet rural backwater expanded from 417 in 1831, to 1,261 ten years later, and by 1851 the census revealed that Wolverton boasted some 2,070 men, women and children who all had to be housed, fed, educated and provided with churches and chapels for Sunday worship. The railway company was a benevolent employer with an attitude that cared for its workforce from 'cradle to grave'. Wolverton was truly the first 'railway town' virtually built from scratch. Once the railway works was up and running, progress was rapid and dramatic. The industrial revolution of the 19th century saw the expansion of

Wolverton to an extent unbelievable to previous generations, and would continue for another one hundred years.

In the early days the directors of the company experienced difficulties in finding accommodation for their workers. The country folk of Old Wolverton did not at first welcome the railways, encouraged in their opposition by the owners of the Grand Junction Canal, who realised they were going to meet fierce competition. This meant that the original workforce had to travel as far as four miles every morning to get to work, as few people living nearer would give them lodgings. But the railway directors were made of sturdy stuff. If the people did not want to offer their men housing, they would build their own, and that is exactly what they did, erecting streets of tiny red-brick two-up, two-down cottages alongside the works, many of which were still lived in until the 1960s, when they were finally demolished.

In July 1841 the first school in Wolverton was opened with the boys paying 2d a week to attend and infants 1d. Later, evening classes were started for the adults as most labouring class men and women in those days were illiterate. Open spaces left between the cottages were made into garden allotments and the families were encouraged to grow their own vegetables.

As the workforce at Wolverton grew it was necessary to recruit men from far afield. In 1844 it was revealed that, attracted by the high wages and the prospect of steady employment, men came from all over Britain. Mechanics came from Scotland and Birmingham, blacksmiths from Wales, carpenters from Manchester and the Isle of Man. Engine fitters who had trained in London left to work in Wolverton and labourers flooded in from Ireland, still in those days, part of Britain.

In order to attract more skilled, white-collar officials (clerks and managers), a small number of semi-detached villas were built near the canal and, as many of the investors in the company were abstaining Quakers, the only two public houses allowed were built outside the Wolverton boundary.

As with many industrial giants of the Victorian age, the London & North Western Railway (as the L&BR had become by then) saw it as a duty to its workers, not only to provide well-paid and stable employment, but to add to the social amenities of the town by giving substantial financial support to churches, schools, sporting facilities and other educational establishments in the area.

They felt their obligations went beyond those of being simply employers and the LNWR was a generous benefactor to the town, but this was not entirely altruistic of course. It was realised that by giving the families of their staff a pleasant environment in which to live and play, they were also going to benefit by having a contented workforce.

Had it not been for the coming of the railway, Wolverton would have remained a rural Buckinghamshire backwater, instead of the thriving, vibrant community it became. Those first workers, who had been 'imported' from many parts of the British Isles, could be described as early 'economic migrants'. Just as today, people were forced to go where the work was available and well paid, and in those days a job on the

BELOW: This view inside the former Royal Train shed at Wolverton Works shows ex-LMSR saloons Nos 798 and 799 immediately after they were retired from service in 1977. (Patrick Kingston)

ABOVE: *Whatever requires attention gets attended to as soon as the Royal Train returns to Wolverton. Here, essential plumbing repairs are carried out in one of the kitchens. (Railcare)*

railways was a secure job for life. Many men spent their entire working lives in the same job – and they were happy to do so.

Wolverton provided a unique opportunity for a stable working life of responsibility, status and regular wages for thousands of men (and later women) who would otherwise never have known them. Prior to moving to Wolverton, where they were taught new skills, they had been farm labourers, foundry and mill workers, quarrymen and navvies, with no job security and precious little chance of promotion. Wolverton and the railway works changed all that.

The massive railway building projects were not welcomed by everyone and 19th century environmentalists claimed (in many cases quite rightly) that the industrialists were despoiling the rural landscape of the countryside purely in the name of profit. But nothing could halt the march of progress and the prospect of good jobs and security for life was too good an opportunity to miss.

The management at Wolverton was in the vanguard of moves to pay more than the going rate in order to attract and keep the right employees. Until the

Wolverton works were up and running, it was common practice in the railway industry to pay engine drivers on a daily basis, which meant that if they did not work, they earned nothing. Consequently, there was no sense of loyalty among the men and this resulted in frequent engine failures. It was Thomas Forsyth, Chief Foreman in the 1840s, who recommended that engine drivers should instead be paid on a contract basis. When this was implemented it saw an immediate benefit in productivity and a dramatic improvement in engine reliability. Forsyth was paid a salary of £400 a year – £8 a week – a very respectable income at a time when £2 was considered a more than decent weekly wage, and any number of men and boys could be found willing to work for £1 a week.

It was on 28 November 1843 that Queen Victoria made her first visit to Wolverton. Accompanied by Prince Albert and the Duke of Wellington, Her Majesty was paying a visit to the man who founded the police force, Sir Robert Peel, at his home, Drayton Manor. The Royal party travelled in the Royal Train from Watford to Tamworth and back and decided to have their luncheon at the new refreshment rooms at Wolverton station. The Queen and Prince Albert again stopped at Wolverton on 15 January 1845 on their way to visit the Duke of Buckingham when two squadrons of the Bucks Yeomanry provided the Guard of Honour and Escort. Queen Victoria made her third and final visit to Wolverton in the 1850s, when, after she had enjoyed an excellent lunch, an enthusiastic crowd was allowed to go through the Royal Luncheon Room and taste what was left of the food.

In 1846 the London & Birmingham Railway merged with several others to form the London & North Western Railway and the new company became a major manufacturer of locomotives and railway carriages.

If it were not for the commercial acuity of the Spencer family, with whom our present Royal Family have had such close relations; not only through the marriage of Lady Diana Spencer to the Prince of Wales in 1981, but also by the fact that her late father, Earl Spencer, was an equerry to both The Queen and her father, King George VI, then Wolverton might not have been able to expand in the way that it did.

successful. Locomotive manufacture continued until September 1863 when the final 'Wolverton Express Goods' No 1075 was delivered. Locomotive overhaul and maintenance was undertaken there for another year. In 1864, the LNWR, which had by now assumed the management of Wolverton, decided to transfer its carriage construction and repair operation from Saltley in Birmingham, to the Buckinghamshire works, thereby giving a welcome vote of confidence to the workers who had naturally been concerned at the loss of locomotive building and the possible effect this would have on their jobs.

However, by 1877 it was decided to concentrate nearly all locomotive production at Crewe, another of the new 'railway' towns (Swindon performed the same role for the rival GWR) and Wolverton would become famous for building and repairing carriages, shortly becoming the largest carriage works in the country, employing more than any other. It was in that same year,

The Radcliffe family owned much of the land surrounding Wolverton and they were not in favour of the large-scale development plans of the LNWR, having already sold the company what they considered to be sufficient land for their needs. So the Spencer family at nearby Althorp, realising the commercial possibilities of having the works and the consequent number of families moving into the area, stepped in and made a financial killing.

Between 1849 and 1862, locomotives were the main product at Wolverton Works with three types of 2-2-2 express engine, the 0-6-0 'Wolverton Goods' engine and the 0-4-2 'Wolverton Tank' engine being the most

1877, that the building, overhaul and maintenance and general care of the LNWR and later LMSR Royal Train coaches (the locomotives are housed elsewhere) was based exclusively at the Wolverton site, which has continued to this day.

It was through the innovations introduced at Wolverton in the 19th century and the early part of the 20th, that many of the comforts later trains, including the Royal Train today, take for granted, became commonplace. In 1873, the first sleeper service from London to Glasgow was introduced, to be extended to Liverpool and Holyhead as boat trains in 1875. In 1889, the LNWR initiated dining cars (for first-class passengers only!) and in 1892 electric lighting on trains was introduced, as were emergency communication cords. So, not content with merely maintaining the status quo, Wolverton continued to seek improvements. At the start of the new century Wolverton became the first railway works in the country to use electricity in its sheds, both for lighting and to drive the heavy machinery, and to crown their position they were selected to build a new Royal Train for King Edward VII in 1903.

Shortly after the end of the First World War, in 1923,

the main railway companies in Britain amalgamated to form the 'Big Four': GWR, Southern Railway, LMSR and LNER. The LNWR management of Wolverton was transferred to the London Midland & Scottish Railway (LMS) and following nationalisation of the railways in 1948, Wolverton became the property of a succession of railway organisations including British Railways, British Rail Engineering, British Rail Maintenance and, following a management buyout, Railcare.

The actual ownership of the Royal Train, the one constant in all these transitions, is unclear as no-one seems quite sure who it is. EWS provides the engines and manpower to run them while Railcare, at Wolverton, looks after the coaches of The Queen and her family. But whether they actually possess the title deeds is another matter, not that anyone is likely to want to sell them – in the present climate – but who knows what 'political necessity' may bring in the future?

A new Royal Train was proposed, to be used by King George VI and Queen Elizabeth just before the Second World War, but before the plans were put into action, wartime restrictions forced a serious rethink. Instead of the luxurious new train that had been envisaged, only

two new saloons were built, one each for The King and Queen. They had identical interiors, with lounge, bedroom, bathroom and valet and maid's quarters. Outside the sides were double-skinned with thick armour plating and splinter-proof glass covering the windows.

In its heyday, Wolverton Works covered 125 acres; today it is just a mere fraction of this, with much of the original site handed over to developers for housing and light industry.

As one would expect, the shed where the Royal Train is housed is immaculate. The concrete floors are swept clear of any grease and dust, and even the rails appear to have been polished – they haven't – it's just an impression one gets. It is also compact in size, when one thinks of some of the earlier works at places such as Swindon. The team is small and dedicated, with fewer than a dozen people working altogether. On the ground floor is a workshop while upstairs is Chris Hillyard's office, which is a treasure trove of Royal railway memorabilia, another office used for meetings and for a secretary and a small canteen where the workers eat their lunch.

Among the key members of the staff are Peter Richardson, the coachbuilder, who has spent a quarter of a century working on the Royal Train, and two electrical fitters, John Best and Geoffrey Garlick, both of whom have 16 years service on the Train behind them.

None of these men is overpaid for their duties on the Royal Train; they do it for their normal wages, but for each of them, it can honestly be said that it is a labour of love. They take an extraordinary pride in working – albeit indirectly – for The Queen and her family, and they know they are appreciated. It is all the reward they want.

Apart from that first visit by Queen Victoria, Wolverton has received Royal visits on a number of occasions. In 1948, just a year after she was married to Prince Philip, Princess Elizabeth (as Duchess of Edinburgh) toured the works facility. A plaque in the works reception area commemorates the occasion. As Queen Elizabeth II, she made her first visit in Coronation Year, 1953, and again in 1977, Silver Jubilee Year, in order to view the new Royal Train coaches that had been built specially for the Jubilee Tour of Great

ABOVE: *Royal saloons Nos 9007 and 9006 are ex-GWR vehicles and were used mainly by Queen Elizabeth, The Queen Mother. No. 9007 was built in 1945 and was mounted on a salvaged war-damaged underframe. It was refurbished in 1948 and modified again in 1955 in order to enlarge Her Majesty's saloon and principal bedroom. No. 9006 was also built in 1945 and, following its second refurbishment in 1955, it contained two bedrooms for the Queen Mother's staff, a bathroom, kitchen and an attendant's sleeping compartment. Both these saloons were transferred to Wolverton from the Western Region in 1962. (Patrick Kingston)*

Britain. It was in April 1998 that Prince Andrew the Duke of York paid his only visit to Wolverton when he undertook a private tour of the railway sheds and inspected the Royal Train coaches.

Wolverton was a tiny country halt that became an early workshop used primarily to repair engines, then a carriage works where some of Britain's most famous and successful railway coaches were built and maintained – and, of course, home to the Royal Train.

Sovereigns from Victoria to Elizabeth II have recognised Wolverton's reputation for excellence. The history of Britain's emergence as one of the truly great industrial nations of the world is reflected in the nearly two centuries' growth of the Wolverton railway works. The worldwide reputation of Wolverton is based on the skill and dedication of the thousands of men and women who worked there since the 1840s. Its apprentice-training scheme was a model followed by industries far beyond Britain's borders and even today is accepted as a term for progressive excellence. Many of the craftsmen who learned their skills at Wolverton travelled to the four corners of the world to work knowing that, 'Wolverton trained' was good enough for anyone.

During two world wars Wolverton played its part with its ambulance trains acknowledged as the most advanced in the world for efficiency and comfort. And it

WOLVERTON WORKS
ESTABLISHED 1838

LONDON & BIRMINGHAM Rly. Co. 1833-1846.   LONDON & NORTH WESTERN Rly. Co. 1846-1922.
LONDON MIDLAND & SCOTTISH Rly. Co. 1923-1947.   BRITISH RAILWAYS 1948.
BRITISH RAIL ENGINEERING LIMITED 1969
BRITISH RAIL MAINTENANCE LIMITED 1987
WOLVERTON RAIL MAINTENANCE LTD. 1994 - RAILCARE WOLVERTON 1995

HER ROYAL HIGHNESS PRINCESS ELIZABETH.
DUCHESS OF EDINBURGH.
visited this Works on 11th March, 1948, and was conducted on a tour of the Works by the Works Superintendent Mr. A. E. Peters.

HER MAJESTY QUEEN ELIZABETH II
AND
HIS ROYAL HIGHNESS PRINCE PHILIP.
DUKE OF EDINBURGH,
visited this Works on 4th April, 1966, and were conducted on a tour of the Works by the Works Manager Mr. Geoffrey Tew.

HER MAJESTY QUEEN ELIZABETH II
again visited this Works on 17th December, 1976, to inspect the new Royal Train Vehicles and was escorted by the Works Manager Mr. W. E. Levett.

ABOVE LEFT AND LEFT: *Two views of Wolverton Works in the 1970s. Some 5,000 men and women were once employed at this famed railway works, but now the total workforce is reduced to just 300, of which fewer than 10 work in the Royal Train sheds. The picture above left shows part of the works' narrow gauge tramway and left is the carriage traverser which moves vehicles from one track to another. (Peter Nicholson)*

Chris Hillyard's office at Wolverton is packed with priceless mementoes and photographs collected in over 30 years of service with the Royal Train. (RAIL magazine)

was during those war years that Wolverton's women responded to the call of the nation, working in the production of shells and aircraft components as well as continuing their peacetime occupations, including making seat covers for the railway's carriages. Their contribution has enhanced the reputation of Wolverton almost as much as their menfolk, certainly in the 20th century.

A visitor to Wolverton today would find it impossible to recognise any part of the original railway works although a large area and several extensive buildings are still in use for railway work. Unlike Swindon, where the outer walls of the workshops have been retained even though nothing is left of the interior, which has been converted into a discount shopping centre, at Wolverton, the Science and Art Museum was destroyed by fire in 1970 and subsequently demolished. The outer walls of the original railway works, started in 1838,

This coach entered service in May 1977 – the Silver Jubilee Year of the Reign of Her Majesty The Queen

BELOW AND RIGHT: *Sir Peter Parker, Chairman of British Rail in 1977, presented this silver key to The Queen on 16 May of that year on the occasion of Her Majesty's first use of her new Royal saloon. The coach, which has a special plaque on the wall, is still in service. (RAIL magazine)*

remained until 1991 but the buildings were then demolished and the site is now used by a giant supermarket, as a car park. So, just as the steam railway forced the closure, in the main, of canal transport in Britain, so now, at Wolverton, the motorcar has triumphed over the locomotive and occupies what was once the proudest citadel of British railway engineering.

There is still a railway maintenance and servicing facility at Wolverton, operating under the Railcare banner, but the once 5,000 strong workforce has been reduced to its present strength of approximately 300. Present day work includes the refurbishment of electric multiple units while the Royal Train and its dedicated band of workers remain to proudly fly the flag first hoisted by Robert Stephenson in October 1836.

CHAPTER 9

The Future

SINCE THE beginning of the reign of Elizabeth II much has changed regarding the Royal Train. Gone are the days when elaborate decorations appeared at every station visited by Royalty and even that essential prerequisite, the red carpet, has all but disappeared apart from one or two State occasions.

Locomotives may still sport cast or enamel Royal coats-of-arms but stationmasters, where they remain, have discarded their top hats and frock coats in favour of the less formal lounge suit. Yet some things never change. All signals along the Royal route still change to green and the operator of the Royal Train takes it as a personal affront if it runs more than 15 seconds early or late.

Stringent security measures in recent years have meant less access by the public when The Queen and her family are expected; not that Her Majesty has asked for this. Indeed, she has let it be known that she is not prepared to live in a cage, no matter how gilded, but in

RIGHT: *The Prince of Wales, a fervent champion of the environment, encouraged the use of 100% biofuel for the Royal Train and travelled on the first journey when they used this more energy-efficient method. The Train is seen here at Scarborough on 14 September 2007. (Geoff Griffiths)*

these matters she realises the difficulties faced by those who are charged with protecting her, and she will not add to their problems as distasteful as it must be to need to be guarded in this way.

Even those who have been fortunate enough to experience such luxury trains as the 'Orient Express' and the 'Flying Scotsman' have never denied that the Royal Train is the ultimate in rail travel in Britain.

The late Princess Margaret once declared that she had never seen a public lavatory when passing through stations on the Royal Train. Not too surprising really, as in those days, anything that might have been considered to be 'offensive' to Royal eyes was covered up or painted over. It doesn't happen anymore. In March 1954,

Princess Margaret also made her one and only journey on an 'ordinary' train when she, accompanied by a large entourage, boarded an InterCity express at Leamington Spa and travelled to Paddington, but the railway officials had made a number of concessions to her Royal status. They attached a Royal saloon, No 9006 to the train, so she did not have to encounter any of the other paying passengers, and an engine named *King George VI*, after her late father, was pulled into service for the occasion.

Whatever the Royal Family does regarding transport, they cannot 'win'. It is a subject that is inevitably surrounded by controversy whether it is the Prince of Wales driving his 'gas-guzzling' Aston Martin or the Princess Royal leasing a top-of-the-range Bentley. The

Queen's use of a £250,000 Rolls-Royce limousine has been attacked as an unnecessary extravagance, even though the vehicle was a gift from the manufacturers on the occasions of Her Majesty's Golden Jubilee in 2002, so did not cost the taxpayers anything, and the previous fleet of Royal cars needed updating anyway.

Similarly, when the Royal Yacht *Britannia* was decommissioned in 1997, there were cries of 'about time too' from critics who claimed the yacht was an anachronism in the 20th century and totally unnecessary for a modern monarch when she could easily reach any part of the globe by air in twenty-four hours. What wasn't generally acknowledged was the fact that *Britannia* had provided a sanctuary for the Queen for over forty years and several feasibility studies had proved that she was worth every penny and, in fact, saved the country millions of pounds during the many overseas tours for which she was used.

When the Government of the day decided that there was no longer a need for The Queen's Flight, and instead, reduced the role to that of a subsidiary squadron, naming it No 32 (The Royal) Squadron thereby attempting (unsuccessfully) to appease Her Majesty with the inclusion of the word 'Royal' – and also making it available to Government ministers for official trips, it was seen as another nail in the coffin of exclusive Royal travel. Opponents of the Monarchy gloated over their victories and the Royal Train became their next target. Of course, it was not difficult to find examples of so-called profligate spending involving the Royal Train considering the small number of times it has been used on an annual basis and the cost of each journey, which has been estimated at over £30,000.

To those opposed to the idea of a Royal Train it appeared to be trying to defend the indefensible and nothing would have persuaded them otherwise. Why couldn't The Queen and her family use public transport like the rest of us? It would save enormous amounts of public money that could be put to much better use. Issues such as security and speed were brushed aside as was the argument that Britain is not some Third World banana republic. So a demonstration was needed to show that the Royal Train is not an uneconomic anachronism anchored in the past, but part of a

modern rail system that is quite prepared to look to the future.

Carbon footprints and climate change are the buzz words of the moment and any way they can be reduced, by flying less, or using cars that do not emit large amounts of carbon dioxide is seen as the only way to save the planet. So when it was announced on 15 September 2007 that the Royal Train had completed its first journey powered entirely by biodiesel fuel that reduced the train's CO_2 emissions by 19 per cent, it proved that the Royal Family were taking seriously the fight against climate change and were in the vanguard of these new improvements. The Royal Household has for some years worked to lower the amount of carbon emitted during transportation to and from Royal engagements and following earlier tests using this type of fuel it was agreed to make this initial experiment. It was an important step towards making all travel by the Royal Train permanently 100 per cent biodiesel powered.

The overnight journey covered some 900 miles between Birmingham and Scarborough and back and Prince Charles wearing his 'environment friendly' hat made rail history by becoming the first member of the Royal Family to travel by rail on this 100 per cent biodiesel-fuelled train. The locomotives that hauled the Royal Train were two Class 67 engines, *Royal Sovereign* and *Queen's Messenger*, top and tailed, operated by English Welsh & Scottish Railway (EWS) who now exclusively arrange all Royal Train travel.

The journey was not some publicity-seeking jaunt by either the railway company or the Royal Family, but a serious effort to determine whether it was possible to power the Royal Train by a fuel-economy method which,

ABOVE: *Before the Palace would agree to the use of 100% biofuel, numerous trials were carried out at EWS's Toton depot in Nottinghamshire, observed on this occasion by Gareth Houghton, EWS Senior Engineer, and Tim Hewlett, Director of Royal Travel, in the cab of a Class 67 locomotive. (Geoff Griffiths)*

FACING PAGE: *This first biofuel Royal Train was an unqualified success on its run to Scarborough from Euston, but 'green' fuels use sustainable ingredients, mainly discarded vegetable oil which can leave the locomotive cab smelling of fish and chips – quite appropriate for a visit to the seaside! (Geoff Griffiths)*

ABOVE: *The Royal Train pauses at York on 22 January 2008, having just dropped off Prince Charles at Malton after an overnight journey from Ayr. It was returning to Scarborough for servicing, before moving to Harrogate to collect the Prince and take him to King's Lynn in Norfolk. (Geoff Griffiths)*

if it was successful, would bode well not only for the future of the train, but for all rail – and other forms of transport.

Therefore, it is worth looking in some detail at that particular journey. The train departed its compound at 19.20 arriving at the Centre Sidings at 08.15. The locomotives, Nos 67005 and 67006 arrived at 20.01 (five seconds early). With No 67005 leading, the Royal Train departed Wolverton at 21.01, exactly on time.

The arrival at Euston was at 22.02 (eight seconds early) with the Prince of Wales and his entourage arriving at 23.23. Three minutes later the train left for an overnight journey to the first night halt, just two seconds late, but by the time they had arrived at the first night halt they were ten seconds early.

After a quiet overnight stop in the allotted stabling sidings, the train departed two seconds early at 06.58 and made a brief stop at York to collect the Operations Manager before proceeding on to Scarborough, where they arrived at 10.17:57 and Driver D. Court of the Doncaster depot correctly positioned the Royal Train within three seconds of 'right time'.

It had been originally planned to operate from Euston

to Scarborough and then from Malton to Andover. However, an outbreak of foot-and-mouth disease had caused a last-minute change of plan and it is testimony to the skill of the train operators that although news of the change was received less than twenty-four hours before the scheduled day of departure, by lunchtime on 13 September all necessary changes to train plan and drivers' diagrams had been made and the Prince of Wales – the client – advised. A further change of part of the plans saw yet another alteration when a security threat at Malton meant the train ran direct to York and Andover. It was while the train was standing at Scarborough that the Train Officer was advised that the TPWS (train protection warning system) cabling for Malton signal 21 (Up Home) had been removed and the British Transport Police treated is as suspicious. The police 'Gold' Control suggested a contingency plan that involved running to Holgate and then picking up in York. The Network Rail Chief Signalling Inspector was consulted and together he and the train officials decided they could get round the problem without being forced to make unscheduled stops at either Weaverthorpe or Malton.

During the layover at Scarborough the Train was

serviced and made ready for a revised departure time of 13.33 to York where it stood at Platform 4 from 14.22 to 14.35. When the Train Officer was informed that Prince Charles's arrival was imminent, the train was moved to the north end of Platform 3 to ensure that the door was correctly positioned for His Royal Highness to entrain. He joined the train at 15.02 and they left York at 15.05 only eight and a half seconds late on the revised time.

Train crew relief took place at Doncaster between 15.30 and 15.32. Further train crew and Network Rail inspector relief at Willesden High Level, the second night stop was reached at Haywards Heath at 21.58 – two seconds early – where the train was shut down for an extended overnight stay.

Next morning the train departed its night halt at 06.35 – on time – with the penultimate train crew relief taking place at Clapham Junction between 08.18 and 08.23.

At Andover, the arrival was scheduled for 10.32 precisely, which 'right time' was reached exactly by Driver S. Bell of Eastleigh. The Prince of Wales and his suite, together with all their luggage had left the train by 10.38 which then departed for Wolverton at 10.41, arriving back at the Royal sheds at 14.02 – 20 seconds early, after a final train crew relief at Kensington Olympia. The entire journey had been undertaken using 100 per cent biofuel for the first time.

So, in spite of the last-minute changes forced by unforeseen circumstances, a diversionary contingency plan had been carried out successfully and the Prince of Wales and his Household had been able to carry out their programme with no disruption to the timetable. Attention to detail is a byword in the Royal Household; for those employed on the Royal Train, it is the eleventh commandment!

Travelling on the Royal Train is a privilege granted to only a few people and the present author found it a rewarding and outstanding experience, which will always provide wonderful memories. The people who work on the Royal Train come into daily contact with the Royal Family on a professional basis and yet none appears to be blasé about the fact. They regard each journey as if it were the first; perhaps this is part of the secret of the success of this remarkable organisation; never to take anything for granted.

The Queen, Prince Philip, the Prince of Wales and the Duchess of Cornwall, all know the hard work that goes into planning and executing every single journey and they appreciate the efforts of everyone involved.

Many of the improvements to rail travel that today's travellers accept as the norm, have come about through Royal train journeys. As has been mentioned in previous chapters, the first lavatory on a train was introduced in a Royal Train, as was the first sleeping carriage (for the Dowager Queen Adelaide in the 1840s), and the first flexible gangway between carriages, which happened in 1869. It was during the reign of King Edward VII that the first, albeit, somewhat rudimentary, air conditioning was introduced, that was in those far off days, little more

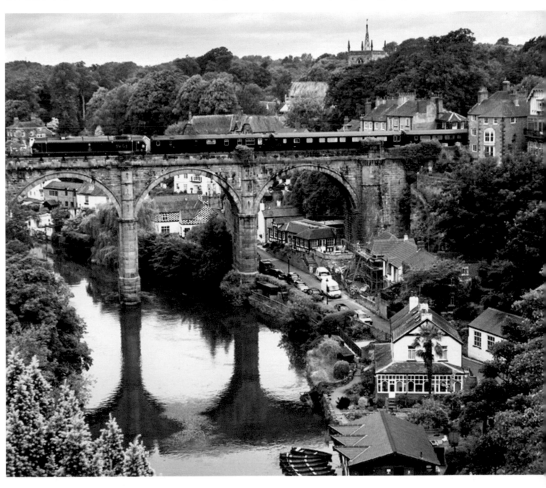

BELOW: *An impressive picture of the Royal Train as it crosses the viaduct at Knaresborough on 10 July 2008. (Geoff Griffiths)*

ABOVE: *The train had left the Prince of Wales at Kirkby Stephen and was returning empty to Wolverton when seen at Garsdale on 31 March 2008. (Geoff Griffiths)*

deemed to be acceptable. The Royal Train is living tribute to the skill and dedication of the engineers and craftsmen who built, and who still maintain, this magnificent example of Royal transport in the 21st century. As we look back to the very beginnings of rail travel by the Royal Family, it would be nice to believe that Queen Victoria, who started it all, would approve of these past 165-odd years of Regal progress.

The Royal Train is not an expensive plaything kept for the sole benefit of an over-privileged family. It is an economically viable form of transport that is supported, not by a dedicated band of die-hard eccentrics for whom railways and anything to do with them are the be all and end all, but by many hard-headed pragmatists who fully understand and accept it is a necessary and integral part of today's Monarchy on the move.

Sir Richard Branson is one of the most successful businessmen in the world with interests in aviation, the media, publishing, insurance and trains. No-one could accuse him of being sentimental when it comes to rail travel, or any other of his many commercial operations. He is a man who puts his money where his mouth is and I asked him for his opinion of the Royal Train, bearing in mind the fact that one of his companies, Virgin Trains, supplies stewards for the Train.

'I am very proud of the fact that so many of our staff are chosen to serve on the Royal Train. The fact that they are is a testament to the rigorous training standards that have seen us leap to the top of the industry in the UK since the introduction of the new Pendolino rolling stock on the West Coast Main Line.

'Long-distance rail travel is booming in the United Kingdom, largely due to the greater speed and frequency of new trains ... and a host of other new services such as Eurostar's new high-speed link to continental Europe. Indeed, Her Majesty has recently travelled on one of our new trains herself when on an official visit north of London.'

The Royal Train enjoys one significant advantage over its competitors in the air and on the roads. It is that it is the only form of transport that is likely to reduce journey times in the future. Experts predict that in twenty years it will be possible for trains to travel at speeds up to 160mph in Britain. Eurostar already reaches speeds in excess of 186mph. So a trip from, say, Aberdeen to

than controlled ventilation. Nevertheless, it was an innovation that was years ahead of its time and had it not been for the willingness of the Sovereign to try out these new ideas, passengers on ordinary scheduled services might have had to wait many more years to experience such facilities.

They did anticipate one monarch in rail comfort though, and that was in the area of dining on board. Passengers (first-class only) travelling between Leeds and London in 1879 were able to enjoy the luxury of luncheon and dinner while on the move, but Queen Victoria refused to have anything to do with this newfangled idea throughout her long life and reign, although a cup of tea was eventually

Penzance could simply be an 'away-day'. And, of course, the Royal Train is still the only 'civilised' way for Royalty to travel from city centre to city centre. Bad weather rarely stops the train, although there may be the odd delay in the autumn with 'leaves on the line'.

The advent of the computer and the subsequent developments in modern technology, have meant changes in transport systems that are almost as dramatic and life-changing this century, as the invention of the internal combustion engine was to the horse-drawn carriage era in the 19th century. The changes taking place throughout the world today will pale in comparison to those we will see in ten years time as we are on the cusp of technological breakthroughs that would have been unimaginable even five years ago.

It may not happen in The Queen's lifetime or even that of the Prince of Wales, but certainly in Prince William's life that day will arrive when every part of the United Kingdom will be a mere couple of hours' journey from any other.

The train is configured very largely for overnight accommodation, although obviously it can, and The Queen does, use it for transit during the day. But in its overnight configuration it does allow her to be in Buckingham Palace during the working week and even have an engagement in the evening before joining the train for an overnight journey to Exeter or Glasgow or wherever she needs to be. She can be there comfortably by 10 o'clock the following morning having had a reasonably good night's sleep, breakfast and still have time to find out who she is going to meet and all the other arrangements and complete a little 'homework' before setting off on another round of engagements. As everyone who works with Her Majesty knows, she is diligent in the extreme in briefing herself before every occasion, and

many people, Prime Ministers included, have found to their cost that it pays to be at least as well-informed as she is. In this day and age, it is a very reasonable way for The Queen, now 82, and Prince Philip 87, to travel and it offers a facility that no other form of transport can.

One thing is certain, the train is here to stay; it is perfect for overnight travel, and if the train did not exist the Royal Household would be forced to find suitable hotels or private houses at considerable public expense and the security problems would be quadrupled. It would also be difficult to take the Queen and her entourage to the more remote places in her realm that she and the Prince of Wales are able to travel to by train. She can always fly to major cities, but using the train does give her the chance to see the more rural and out of the way parts of the United Kingdom, which would be almost impossible otherwise.

The carriages maybe getting old (after all, they are Mark 3s) but they are acknowledged throughout the rail industry as being extremely well designed, beautifully built and likely to be around for a long time. They are looked after very carefully as you would expect, and kept in pristine condition, and obviously they don't cover the same amount of mileage as commercial vehicles. So there is still plenty of life left in the Royal Train and The Queen will continue to use it for as long as she wishes, and the Prince of Wales will do the same.

The future for rail travel, and for the Royal Train in particular, is very bright. If those people who continually try to downgrade the Monarchy, will leave the running of the Royal Train to those who really do know what they are doing, it will continue to enhance the status of Britain's Royal Family, and therefore the reputation of the country, well into the second half of the 21st century.

Appendix

ROYAL TRAIN SCHEDULES 1838–2002

1838–1841
FIRST ROYAL TRAIN SCHEDULE
page 158

1901
QUEEN VICTORIA'S FUNERAL TRAIN YEAR
page 158

1910
ROYAL TRAIN SCHEDULE
page 160

1936
KING GEORGE V FUNERAL TRAIN YEAR
page 161

1947
KING GEORGE VI'S ROYAL TRAINS
page 162

1952
KING GEORGE VI FUNERAL TRAIN YEAR
page 164

1977
SILVER JUBILEE ROYAL TRAINS
page 167

1997
INCLUDING DIANA, PRINCESS OF WALES FUNERAL TRAIN
page 170

2002
GOLDEN JUBILEE TOUR YEAR
page 172

RIGHT: *A spotless GWR No. 3373*
Royal Sovereign *waiting to carry*
Queen Victoria's coffin. (Getty Images)

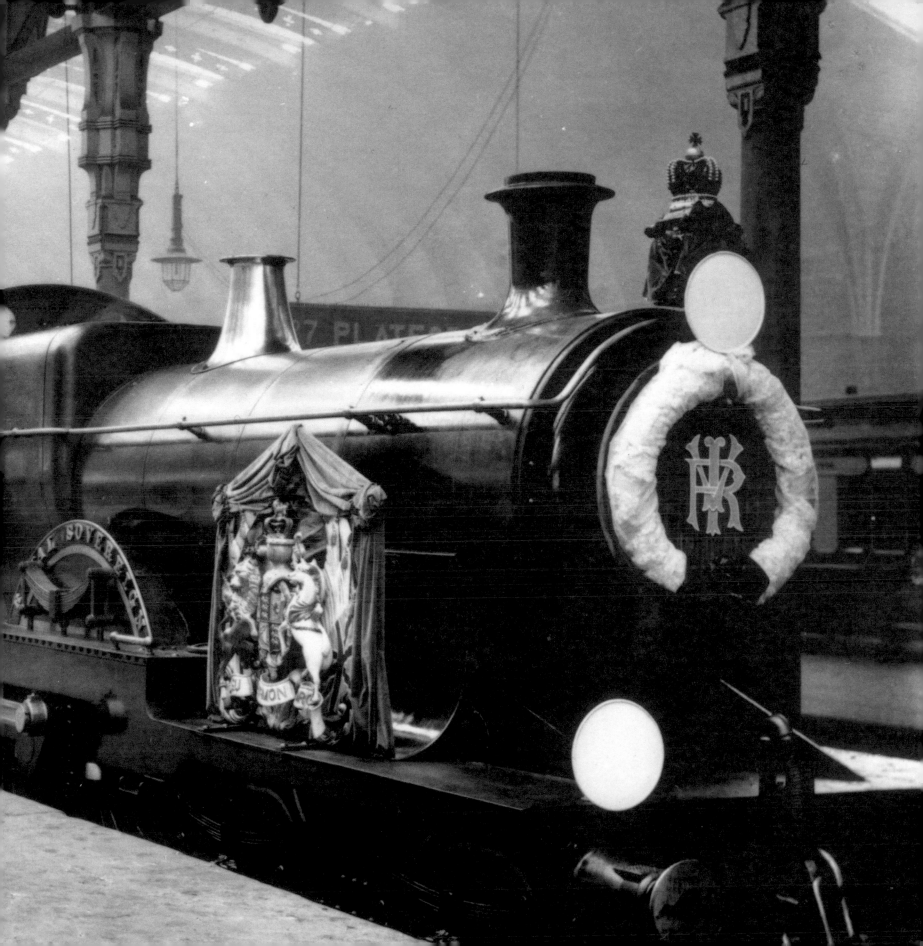

1838–1841
FIRST ROYAL TRAIN SCHEDULE

1838–1841	MEMBER OF THE ROYAL FAMILY	JOURNEY DETAILS	RAILWAY	STOCK
14 November 1839	HRH Prince Albert HRH Prince Ernst of Saxe-Coburg-Gotha (HRH Prince Albert's first train journey.)	Slough–London Paddington	GWR	GWR
22 July 1840	HM Queen Adelaide	Nottingham–Leeds	North Midland Railway	L&BR (3 carriages + 4 trucks) NMR saloon

1901
QUEEN VICTORIA'S FUNERAL TRAIN YEAR

1901	MEMBER OF THE ROYAL FAMILY	JOURNEY DETAILS	RAILWAY	STOCK
18 January	HRH The Prince of Wales	Ballater–London Euston	LNWR	LNWR
19 January	HRH The Prince of Wales	London Victoria–Portsmouth	LBSCR	LBSCR
21 January	HRH The Prince of Wales German Kaiser	Portsmouth Dockyard–London Victoria	LBSCR	LBSCR
23 January	HM King Edward VII	London Victoria–Portsmouth Dockyard	LBSCR	LBSCR
24 January	HRH The Duke of York HRH The Duke of Connaught	London–Portsmouth Dockyard	LBSCR	LBSCR
1 February	HM King Edward VII	Portsmouth Dockyard–London Victoria	LBSCR	LB SCR
2 February	The Emperor of Germany Royal Princes	Gosport Clarence Yard–London Victoria LSWR A12 class No 555 LBSCR B4 class No 54 *Empress* LBSCR B4 class No 53 *Sirdar* (Funeral train of HM Queen Victoria)	LSWR LBSCR	LBSCR (7) + GWR saloon 229
2 February	King Edward VII Members of the Royal Family	London Paddington–Windsor No 3050 *Royal Sovereign* (No 3373 *Atbara* renamed and numbered for the occasion) (Funeral train of HM Queen Victoria)	GWR	GWR saloon 229 2 x Royal saloons 1st class corridor coach, 2 x vans
5 February	The Emperor of Germany and guests	Windsor–London Paddington	GWR	GWR
5 February	HM King Edward VII	London Paddington–Windsor	GWR	GWR
7 February	HM King Edward VII – HM Queen Alexandra	Windsor–London Paddington	GWR	GWR
16 February	?	London Paddington–Windsor	GWR	GWR
18 February	?	Windsor–London Paddington	GWR	GWR

1901 continued	MEMBER OF THE ROYAL FAMILY	JOURNEY DETAILS	RAILWAY	STOCK
? March	HM King Edward VII TRH The Duke and Duchess of York	London Victoria–Portsmouth Dockyard (Duke and Duchess boarded SS *Ophir*)	LBSCR	LBSCR
? March	HM King Edward VII – HM Queen Alexandra TRH The Duke and Duchess of Cornwall	London Waterloo–Portsmouth Harbour Portsmouth Harbour–London Waterloo	LSWR	LSWR
22/23 March	HM Queen Alexandra	Calais–Copenhagen		L&SER saloon No 1
30 March	?	London Paddington–Windsor	GWR	GWR
9 April	?	Windsor–London Paddington London Paddington–Windsor	GWR	GWR
9/10 April	HM Queen Alexandra *HIM The Dowager Empress of Russia	*Copenhagen–Fredericia Neumienster–Frankfurt Frankfurt–Cronberg (HM travelled in the Russian Imperial train– Fredericia–Neumienster)		L&SER saloon No 1
13/14 April	HM Queen Alexandra	Cronberg–Frankfurt Frankfurt–Calais		L&SER saloon No 1
13 April	?	Windsor–London Paddington	GWR	GWR
14 April	HM Queen Alexandra	Frankfurt–Calais		L&SER saloon No 1
25 May	?	London Paddington–Windsor	GWR	GWR
12 July	HM King Edward VII	London Euston–Whitmore (147 miles)	LNWR	LNWR
15 July	HM King Edward VII	Whitmore–London Euston (147 miles)	LNWR	LNWR
27/28 September	HM King Edward VII HM Queen Alexandra	London Euston–Ballater (583 miles)	LNWR North British Railway Caledonian Railway Great North of Scotland Railway	210, 870, 72, 73, 59, 50; Royal saloons 56, 9, 180, 306, 272
21/22 October	HM King Edward VII HM Queen Alexandra HRH Princess Victoria of Wales TRH The Prince and Princess of York TRH The Prince and Princess of Cornwall	Ballater–London Euston (583 miles)	Caledonian Railway North British Railway Great North of Scotland Railway LNWR	210, 870, 72, 73, 59, 50; Royal saloons 56, 9, 180, 306, 272
1 November	TRH The Duke and Duchess of York	Portsmouth Dockyard–London Victoria LBSCR B4 class No 54 *Empress* (TRH return from world tour)	LBSCR	LBSCR

1910

Date	Member of the Royal Family	Journey details	Railway	Stock
21 January	HM Queen Alexandra TRH The Prince and Princess of Wales	Wolferton–Windsor	Great Eastern Railway	GER
21 January	HM King Edward VII	London Paddington–Windsor	GWR	GWR
6–9 March	HM King Edward VII	London Victoria–Dover Calais–Paris Paris–Biarritz	SECR	SECR
14 April	HM Queen Alexandra – HRH Princess Victoria (HM and HRH to Genoa and Corfu)	London Victoria–Portsmouth Dockyard	LBSCR	LBSCR
26/27 April	HM King Edward VII	Biarritz–Calais Calais–London Victoria (HM's final Continental journey)	SECR	SECR
20 May		London Paddington–Windsor (Funeral of King Edward – died 6 May)	GWR	GWR
24 June	HM King George V – HM Queen Mary	London Paddington–Windsor	GWR	GWR
21 July	HM King George V – HM Queen Mary	? –Portsmouth Dockyard (TM on Naval tour)		
29 July	HM King George V – HM Queen Mary	Torquay–London Paddington	GWR	GWR
8/9 August	HM King George V – HM Queen Mary	London Euston–Ballater (583 miles) LNWR Nos 2663 *George the Fifth* and 2664 *Queen Mary* GNSR No 31	LNWR	LNWR No 12
19 September	HM Queen Alexandra	Ballater–Dundee (HM joins RY for Copenhagen; last GNSR RT working)	GNSR	GNSR
11 October	HM King George V – HM Queen Mary	Ballater–London Euston (583 miles)	LNWR	LNWR
22 October	HM King George V – HM Queen Mary	London Paddington–Evesham Evesham–London Paddington	GWR	LNWR
26 October	HM King George V – HM Queen Mary	London Paddington–Windsor Windsor–London Paddington (Funeral of Prince Francis of Teck)	GWR	GWR
28 October	HM King George V – HM Queen Mary	London Paddington–Evesham Evesham–London Paddington	GWR	LNWR
19 November	HM King George V – HM Queen Mary	Wolferton–Windsor	GER	GER
28 November	HM King George V	Windsor–London Paddington	GWR	GWR
28 November	HM Queen Mary	Windsor–Wolferton	GER	GER
? December	Turkish leaders	London Victoria–Portsmouth Dockyard H1 class No 37	LBSCR	LBSCR

1936
KING GEORGE V FUNERAL TRAIN YEAR

Date	Member of the Royal Family	Journey details	Railway	Stock
23 January		Wolferton–London King's Cross B12 class No 8520 B17 class No 2847 *Helmingham Hall* (HM's mortal remains brought to London)	LNER	LNER brake 1st 4188, 1st class saloon 41280, 1st class saloon 43099, saloons 46, 395, 396, 1st class saloon 43100, 1st class saloons 41281, 109
27 January	HM The King of Rumania	Dover Marine–London Victoria	Southern Railway	SR van 2335, Pullmans *Lady Dalziel, Cecilia* brake 7747
27 January	HE The President of France	Dover Marine–London Victoria	Southern Railway	SR van 2353, Pullmans *Minerva, Fingall,* *Rosemary,* brake 7749
27 January	HM The King of the Belgians	Dover Marine–London Victoria	Southern	SR van 2344, Pullman *Diamond,* brake 7752
28 January	HM King Edward VIII – HM Queen Mary	London Paddington–Windsor Windsor–London Paddington No 4082 *Windsor Castle* (Funeral of HM George V at Windsor)	GWR	GWR brake 1st 4188, 1st class saloons 41280, 43099, saloons 46, 395, 396, 1st class saloons 43100, 41281, 109.
28 January	Royal Mourners	London Paddington–Windsor No 4090 *Dorchester Castle* (Funeral of HM George V at Windsor)	GWR	
19 May	?	London Victoria–Portsmouth Harbour T9 class No 716	Southern Railway	SR 7914 7930, 7920, 7254, 7915
8–10 August	The Maharajah of Mysore	London Victoria–Portsmouth Southsea–Torquay Torquay–Bristol T9 class No 122	Southern Railway GWR	LNWR
19 September	HM King Edward VIII – HRH The Duke of York	? –BALLATER	LMSR	LNWR
30 September–1 October	HM King Edward VIII TRH The Duke and Duchess of Kent	Ballater–London	LMSR	LNWR
11 October	HM King Edward VIII	Portsmouth Dockyard–London Victoria B4 class No 46 *Prince of Wales*	Southern Railway	LBSCR
18/19 November	HM King Edward VIII	London Paddington–Llantwit Major Usk–Cwmbran Rhymney–London Paddington GWR 2-6-2T No 4110 (HM Abdicated on 10 December)	GWR	GWR 9004, 9005, 1 x sleeping car, ? x 1st class cars
30 November	HRH The Duke of York	London Euston–Edinburgh	LMSR	
2 December	HRH The Duke of York	Edinburgh–London Euston	LMSR	

1947
KING GEORGE VI'S ROYAL TRAINS

DATE	MEMBER OF THE ROYAL FAMILY	JOURNEY DETAILS	RAILWAY	STOCK

31 January	HM King George VI – HM Queen Elizabeth
	
	**HM Queen Mary
	HRH Princess Elizabeth
	HRH Princess Margaret
		London Waterloo (or Victoria)
		  –Portsmouth Harbour
		**Portsmouth Harbour–London Victoria
		No 850 *Lord Nelson*
		(TMs to join HMS *Vanguard* en route to
		  South Africa)
			Southern Railway	Pullmans *Aurora,*
				Plato, Rosemary,
				Medusa, Juno

11 May	HRH The Duke of Gloucester	London Victoria –Portsmouth Harbour No 850 *Lord Nelson*	Southern Railway	?
12 May	HM King George VI – HM Queen Elizabeth HRH Princess Elizabeth HRH Princess Margaret HRH The Duke of Gloucester	Portsmouth Harbour–London Waterloo (74 miles) No 850 *Lord Nelson* No 799 *Sir Ironside* (pilot loco) No 777 *Sir Lamiel* (standby) (TM's return from South Africa)	Southern Railway	Pullmans *Aurora,* *Plato, Rosemary,* *Medusa, Juno*
3 June	HM King George VI – HM Queen Elizabeth	London King's Cross–Cambridge Cambridge–London King's Cross B2 class No 1671 *Royal Sovereign*	LNER	LNER 109, ?, 395, 396, ?, ?
7 June	HM King George VI – HM Queen Elizabeth	London Victoria–Tattenham Corner No 21C157 *Biggin Hill* (TM attend The Derby)	Southern Railway	Pullman?
25/26 June	HM King George VI – HM Queen Elizabeth	London King's Cross–Norwich Thorpe Norwich Thorpe–Wolverton (420? miles)	LNER	5155, 805, 799, 798, 76, 807, 477, 806, 77, 5154
14/15 July	HM King George VI – HM Queen Elizabeth HRH Princess Elizabeth HRH Princess Margaret	London Euston–Edinburgh (497? miles)	LMSR	5155, 461, 805, 799, 798, 76, 807, 495, 477, 806, 77, 5154
21/25 July	HM King George VI – HM Queen Elizabeth HRH Princess Elizabeth HRH Princess Margaret	Edinburgh–Glasgow Ibrox–Greenock Upper Port Glasgow–Greenock Greenock–Wemyss Bay Wemyss Bay–London Euston (767? miles)	LMSR	5155, 461, 805, 799, 798, 76, 807, 495, 806, 77, 5154
8/10 August	HM King George VI – HM Queen Elizabeth HRH Princess Elizabeth HRH Princess Margaret	London Euston–Ballater (583 miles)	LMSR	5155, 461, 805, 798, 76, 807, 495,477, 806, 77, 5154
28/29 September	HM King George VI HRH Princess Elizabeth HRH Princess Margaret HRH The Duke of Gloucester	Ballater–London Euston (583 miles)	LMSR	5155, 461, 805, 800 801, 76, 807, 495, 477, 806, 77, 5154
12/13 October	HM King George VI – HM Queen Elizabeth	Ballater–London Euston (583 miles)	LMSR	5155, 805, 799, 798, 76, 807, 495, 806, 77, 477, 5154

1947 *continued*	MEMBER OF THE ROYAL FAMILY	JOURNEY DETAILS	RAILWAY	STOCK
28/31 October	HM King George VI – HM Queen Elizabeth HRH Princess Elizabeth	London Paddington–St Austell Devonport–Kingswear Kingswear–London Paddington (667? miles) Nos 5069 *Isambard Kingdom Brunel* and 5055 *Earl of Eldon* 5094 *Tretower Castle* 7818 *Granville Manor* 6838 *Goodmoor Grange* and 2-6-0 No 5318 No 5058 *Earl of Clancarty* 2-6-2Ts Nos 5150 and 5113 (First journeys of saloons 798 and 799 following removal of wartime armour plate and repainting)	GWR	5155, 805, 799, 798, 76, 807, 495, 806, 77, 477, 5154
20 November	HRH Princess Elizabeth HRH Prince Philip of Greece	London Waterloo–Winchester (66? miles) Nos 857 *Lord Howe* 766 *Sir Geraint* 785 *Sir Mador de la Porte* 850 *Lord Nelson* M7 class No 249 (TRH begin Honeymoon)	Southern Railway	Corridor 3rd brake, corridor compo, Pullmans *Rosemary*, *Rosamund*, corridor 3rd brake

Note: last visit of Royal Train to Bolton Abbey recorded as October 1947

1952
KING GEORGE VI FUNERAL TRAIN YEAR

DATE	MEMBER OF THE ROYAL FAMILY	JOURNEY DETAILS	BR REGION	STOCK
11 February	?	Wolferton–London King's Cross Nos 61617 *Ford Castle* 70000 *Britannia* (King George VI's mortal remains to London)	Eastern	1541, 41280, 46, 396, 395, 43099, 41281, 109
14 February	HRH Prince Albert of Belgium	Dover Marine–London Victoria Nos 30919 *Harrow* 34071 601 *Squadron* 30766 *Sir Geraint*	Southern	
15 February	HM Queen Elizabeth II HM The Queen Mother HRH Princess Margaret HRH The Princess Royal	London Paddington–Windsor No 4082 *Windsor Castle* (No 7013 *Bristol Castle* renumbered and renamed for the occasion) (Funeral of HM King George VI at Windsor)	Western	1541, 41280, 46, 396, 395, 43099, 41281, 109
16 February	HRH Prince Albert of Belgium Prince Felix and Grand Duchess Charlotte of Luxembourg	London Victoria–Dover Marine Nos 30919 *Harrow* 30766 *Sir Geraint*	Southern	Pullmans *Juno, Penelope, Cygnus, Malaga, Montana,* van 2341
17 February	HM The King of Denmark	London Victoria–Dover Marine No 34071 601 *Squadron*	Southern	Brake 2nd, compo, Pullmans *Chloria, Montana,* brake 3rd
29 February	HM King Paul of Greece	? No 34071 601 *Squadron*	Southern	
2/3 April	HRH The Duke of Edinburgh	London Euston–Lowton Lowton–Crewe Crewe–London Euston (504 miles)	London Midland	5154, 45006, 45005, 45000
7/8 May	?	London Paddington–Swansea Swansea–Margam Margam–London Paddington Nos 7032 *Denbigh Castle* 6903 *Belmont Hall* (Operated under 'Deepdene' conditions attached to service trains)	Western	7372, 9093, 9005, 9007, 9006, 7377
26/27 May	HM Queen Elizabeth II HRH The Duke of Edinburgh HRH The Duke of Cornwall HRH Princess Anne	London Euston–Ballater (635? miles)	London Midland Scottish	5155, 461, 805, 799, 798, 76, 807, 495, 477, 806, 77, 5154
6 June	HM Queen Elizabeth II HRH The Duke of Edinburgh	London Victoria–Tattenham Corner No 30915 *Brighton*	Southern	?
15/16 June	HRH The Duke of Cornwall HRH Princess Anne	Ballater–London Euston (399? miles)	Scottish London Midland	5155, 461, 805, 799, 798, 76, 807, 495, 477, 806, 77, 5154

1952 continued	MEMBER OF THE ROYAL FAMILY	JOURNEY DETAILS	RAILWAY	STOCK
17 June	?	Ballater–London Euston (Vehicles attached to service train at Perth)	Scottish Midland London	Brake,corridor 1st, sleeper 387, restaurant 1st
24/25 June	HM Queen Elizabeth II	London Euston–Edinburgh (399? miles)	London Midland Scottish	5155, 461, 805, 799, 798, 76, 807, 495, 477, 806, 77, 5154
24 June	HRH Princess Margaret	London Waterloo–Portsmouth Town *Portsmouth Town–London Waterloo	Southern	2 x 4-COR emu and 1 x 4-car restaurant emu *1 x 4-COR emu and 2 x 4-car restaurant emu
30 June/1 July	HM Queen Elizabeth II	Edinburgh–London Euston (489? miles)	Scottish London Midland	5155, 461, 805, 799, 76, 807, 495, 806, 77, 477, 5154
1/3 July	HM Queen Elizabeth II	London Paddington–Newton Abbot Newton Abbot–Dorchester West Dorchester West–Gillingham Salisbury–London Waterloo (489? miles) Nos 6018 *King Henry VI* 7809 *Childrey Manor* 7801 *Anthony Manor* 7806 *Cockington Manor* 7014 *Caerhays Castle* 7015 *Carn Brea Castle* 5985 *Mostyn Hall* 35025 *Brocklebank Line* N class 2-6-0s Nos 31841 and 31831 35023 *Holland Afrika Line* 35015 *Rotterdam Lloyd* 35001 *Channel Packet*	Western Southern	5155, 45005, 387, 799, 798, 76, 807, 495, 477, 806, 77, 5154
7/8 August	HM Queen Elizabeth II HRH The Duke of Edinburgh HRH The Duke of Cornwall HRH Princess Anne	London Euston–Ballater (1,167? miles) No 46229 *Duchess of Hamilton* Class 5 4-60s Nos 45020 (stand-by at Rugby) 44670 and 44674	London Midland Scottish	5155, 461, 805, 799, 798, 76, 807, 495, 477, 806, 77, 5154
7/8 August	TRH The Duke and Duchess of Kent	London King's Cross–Aberdeen (Coach attached to down 'Night Aberdonian')	North Eastern Eastern Scottish	?
12/14 September	HM Queen Elizabeth II	Ballater–Bawtry Bawtry–Ballater (956? miles)	Scottish North Eastern Eastern	5155, 45005, 799, 76, 807, 495, 806, 77, 5154
13/14 October	HM Queen Elizabeth II HRH Prince Charles HRH Princess Anne HRH Princess Margaret	Ballater–London Euston (1,167? miles) No 46245 *City of London*	Scottish London Midland	5155, 30400, 45005, 387, 799, 76, 807, 495, 477, 806, 77, 5154
21 October	HRH The Duke of Edinburgh	London Waterloo–Portsmouth Portsmouth–London Waterloo	Southern	

1952 *continued*	MEMBER OF THE ROYAL FAMILY	JOURNEY DETAILS	RAILWAY	STOCK
22/24 October	HM Queen Elizabeth II HRH The Duke of Edinburgh	London Paddington–Llandrindod Wells Llandrindod Wells–Shrewsbury Shrewsbury–London Paddington (516 miles) Nos 7030 *Cranbrook Castle* 7036 *Taunton Castle* 7913 *Little Wyrley Hall* 6971 *Athelhampton Hall* 6976 *Graythwaite Hall*	Western	5155, 45005, 799, 798, 76, 807, 495, 806, 77, 477, 5154
28/31 October		London Paddington–Minehead Minehead–Plymouth (Millbay) Plymouth (Millbay)–Penzance Penzance–Taunton No 7030 *Cranbrook Castle* 2-6-0 No 5376	Western	7372, 9007, 9006, 9086, 9005, 7377
21 November	HM Queen Elizabeth II	London Waterloo–Fort Brockenhurst Fareham–London Waterloo Nos 34011 *Tavistock* 34020 *Seaton* (HM presents new colours to HMS *Daedalus*)	Southern	Pullmans *Minerva, Orion, Phoenix, Aires, Isle of Thanet*
25/28 November	HRH Princess Margaret	London King's Cross–Newcastle (611? miles)	Eastern North Eastern	45005, 45006, 5154
28 November	HRH Princess Margaret	Newcastle–Peterborough	North Eastern Eastern	109, 395, 396

1959

1959	MEMBER OF THE ROYAL FAMILY	JOURNEY DETAILS	RAILWAY	STOCK
6/7 August	HM Queen Elizabeth II HRH The Duke of Edinburgh HRH Prince Charles HRH Princess Anne	London Euston–Ballater	British Railways (Midland)	5155, 80918, 45005, 2900, 799, 798, 499, 2901 495, 477, 806, 77 31209, 635

1977
SILVER JUBILEE ROYAL TRAINS

DATE	MEMBER OF THE ROYAL FAMILY/ HEAD OF STATE	JOURNEY DETAILS	RAILWAY OPERATOR	STOCK
3/4 February	HRH The Prince of Wales	London Paddington–Pontypridd (470 miles)	British Rail	5155, 45005, 9006, 31209
26/27 April	HRH The Princess Anne	London Euston–Stoke-on-Trent Stoke-on-Trent–Slough (422 miles) Class 25s Nos 25218 and 25057	British Rail	5155, 45005, 9006, 31209
2/3 May	HM Queen Elizabeth II HRH The Duke of Edinburgh	London Euston–Barrow (538 miles) Class 40s Nos 40025 and 40109	British Rail	5155, 324, SLS2620, 45005, 798, 799, 9006, 31209
16/20 May	HM Queen Elizabeth II HRH The Duke of Edinburgh	London Euston–Glasgow Central Glasgow Central–Stirling Stirling–Perth Perth–Dundee Aberdeen–Edinburgh (1,310 miles) Nos 87004 47424 47550 (First Silver Jubilee tour)	British Rail	2906, 2903, 2904, 2902, 2901, 2900, 2013, 45000, 325, 2905
17/19 May	HRH The Prince of Wales	Plymouth–Penrith Penrith– Oxenholme Oxenholme–Lowton Lowton–London Euston (1,003 miles)	British Rail	5155, 45005, 9006, 31209
31 May/1 June	HM Queen Elizabeth II HRH The Duke of Edinburgh HM Queen Elizabeth the Queen Mother TRH The Duke & Duchess of Kent HRH Princess Alexandra	London Victoria–Tattenham Corner (164 miles) Nos 25177and 31414 Stand-by 31416 and 73103 33014 and 25069	British Rail	5155, 324, 396, 5155
2/3 June	HRH The Prince of Wales	London Euston–Welshpool (660 miles)	British Rail	5155, 45005, 9006, 5154
9/10 June	HRH The Prince of Wales	London Paddington–Bodmin Road (270 miles)	British Rail	5155, 45005, 9006, 5154
19/22 June	HM Queen Elizabeth II HRH The Duke of Edinburgh	Slough–Lancaster Preston–Wigan Wigan–Manchester Hazel Grove–Liverpool Porthmadog–Harlech (706 miles) Nos 87004 47455 47491 25221 and 25222 25218	British Rail	2906, 2903, 2904, 2902, 2901, 2900, 2013, 45000, 325, 2905
22/23 June	HM Queen Elizabeth the Queen Mother	London King's Cross–Dalmeny Edinburgh–London Euston (972 miles)	British Rail	5155, 9007, 45005, 9006, 31209

1977 *continued*	MEMBER OF THE ROYAL FAMILY/ HEAD OF STATE	JOURNEY DETAILS	RAILWAY OPERATOR	STOCK
26/27 June	HRH The Prince of Wales	Reading–Wrexham (450 miles)	British Rail	5155, 45005, 9006, 5154
27 June	HM Queen Elizabeth II HRH The Duke of Edinburgh	Windsor–Portsmouth Harbour (Fleet Review 28 June)	British Rail	4-BEP emu 7020
29 June	HM Queen Elizabeth II HRH The Duke of Edinburgh	Portsmouth Harbour–London Waterloo	British Rail	4-BEP emu 7020
12/13 July	HM Queen Elizabeth II HRH The Duke of Edinburgh	Barnsley–Leeds Leeds–Wakefield Westgate (355 miles) Nos 47527 47155	British Rail	2906, 2903, 2904, 2902, 2901, 2900, 2013, 45000, 325, 2905
14/16 July	HRH The Prince of Wales	London Euston–Rugeley Stoke-on-Trent–Slough (444 miles)	British Rail	2906, 2901, 45000, 2905
14/15 July	HM Queen Elizabeth the Queen Mother	London King's Cross–Dundee	British Rail	5155, 9007, 45005, 9006, 5154
21/22 July	HRH The Duke of Edinburgh	London Euston–Leicester (210 miles)	British Rail	2906, 2904, 2900, 2905
21/22 July	HRH The Prince of Wales	London Paddington–Carmarthen (566 miles) Nos 31414 and 31416	British Rail	5155, 45005, 9006, 5154
26/29 July	HM Queen Elizabeth II	London Euston–Bushbury HRH The Duke of Edinburgh Coventry–Birmingham International Birmingham International–Derby Nottingham–Finningley (620 miles) Nos 87004 87007 (standby) 47545 47529 47514	British Rail	2906, 2903, 2904, 2902, 2901, 2900, 2013, 45000, 325, 2905
26/27 July	HRH Princess Anne	Newcastle–Dumfries (754 miles) Nos 25221 and 25222	British Rail	5154, 9006, 45005, 5155
8 August	HM Queen Elizabeth II HRH The Duke of Edinburgh	Bristol–Bath Keynsham–Weston-super-Mare No 253025	British Rail (Western)	High Speed Train
9/10 September	HRH The Prince of Wales	Aberdeen–Aberdare (1,220 miles)	British Rail	2906, 2901, 45000, 2905
12/13 September	HRH The Prince of Wales	London Euston–Aberdeen (1,002 miles)	British Rail	2906, 2901, 45000, 2905
17/19 September	HM Queen Elizabeth II	Aberdeen–London King's Cross No 31401 (Peterborough–King's Cross) (1,167 miles)	British Rail	5155, 9007, 80728, SLE2120

1977 *continued*	MEMBER OF THE ROYAL FAMILY/ HEAD OF STATE	JOURNEY DETAILS	RAILWAY OPERATOR	STOCK
23/25 September	HRH The Prince of Wales	Aberdeen–Llanelli Cardiff–Aberdeen (2,204 miles) No 87004	British Rail	2906, 2901, 45000, 2905
10/11 October	HM Queen Elizabeth II	Aberdeen–London Euston (1,082 miles)	British Rail	2906, 2903, 2902, 2901, 2900, 2013, 45000, 325, 2905
24/25 November	HRH The Prince of Wales	London Euston–Uttoxeter Chester–Mold Mold–Chester (358 miles)	British Rail	2906, 2901, 45000, 2905
2/3 December	HRH The Prince of Wales	Llanelli–Swansea Swansea–Salisbury (572 miles)	British Rail	2906, 2901, 45000, 2905
13/15 December	HRH The Prince of Wales	London Euston–Ashton Bolton St Trinity–London Euston (450 miles)	British Rail	2906, 2901, 45000, 2905

Note: No 40109 on Royal Train during June, no further information available

1997
INCLUDING DIANA, PRINCESS OF WALES FUNERAL TRAIN

Date	Member of the Royal Family/ Head of State	Journey details	Railway operator	Stock
23/34 January	HRH The Prince of Wales	King's Lynn–Newcastle (712 miles) Nos 47798 *Prince William* 37057	EWS	2906, 2922, 2923, 2919, 2915, 2920
25 February	The President of Israel HRH The Duke of York	London Victoria–Gatwick Airport Gatwick Airport–London Victoria (177 miles) Nos 47798 *Prince William* 73131 73128 (State visit)	EWS	2921, 2917, 2918, 2916, 2920, 2915
20/21 March	HM Queen Elizabeth II	London Euston–Mansfield Town (455 miles) Nos 47798 *Prince William* 37109	EWS	2906, 2903, 2916, 2918, 2914, 2917, 2915, 2920
24/25 March	HRH The Prince of Wales	London Euston–Barry Town (460 miles) Nos 86216 *Meteor* 47798 *Prince William* 47799 *Prince Henry*	EWS	2906, 2922, 2923, 2919, 2915, 2920
26/27 March	HM Queen Elizabeth II HRH The Duke of Edinburgh	London Euston–Bradford Forster Square (555 miles) Nos 47798 *Prince William* 47799 *Prince Henry*	EWS	2906, 2903, 2904, 2918, 2914, 2917, 2915, 2920
6/7 April	HRH The Prince of Wales	Kemble–Aberdeen (1,198 miles) No 47798 *Prince William*	EWS	2906, 2922, 2923, 2919, 2915, 2920
9/10 April	HM Queen Elizabeth II	Slough–Totnes (538 miles) No 47798 *Prince William*	EWS	2906, 2903, 2916, 2918, 2914, 2917, 2915, 2920
23/24 April	HRH The Prince of Wales	London Euston–Cardiff Central (414 miles) Nos 47798 *Prince William* 47782	EWS	2906, 2922, 2923, 2919, 2915, 2920
08/09 May	HM Queen Elizabeth II HRH The Duke of Edinburgh	London Euston–Cogan (419 miles) Nos 47798 *Prince William* 47799 *Prince Henry*	EWS	2906, 2903, 2904, 2918, 2914, 2917, 2915, 2920
22/23 May	HM Queen Elizabeth II HRH The Duke of Edinburgh	London Euston–Heworth (670 miles) No 47798 *Prince William*	EWS	2906, 2903, 2904, 2918, 2914, 2917, 2915, 2920
4/5 June	HRH The Prince of Wales	London Euston–Middlesbrough (661 miles) Nos 90018 47799 *Prince Henry*	EWS	2921, 2922, 2923, 2919, 2915, 2920
7 June	HM Queen Elizabeth II HM Queen Elizabeth the Queen Mother TRH Prince & Princess Michael of Kent	London Victoria–Tattenham Corner (149 miles) Nos 47798 *Prince William* 47799 *Prince Henry*	EWS	2921, 2916, 2918, 2917, 2905

1997 *continued*	MEMBER OF THE ROYAL FAMILY/ HEAD OF STATE	JOURNEY DETAILS	RAILWAY OPERATOR	STOCK
8–10 June	HRH The Prince of Wales	Kemble–Bodmin Parkway Pontsmill–Taunton (757 miles) Nos 47798 *Prince William* 47799 *Prince Henry*	EWS	2921, 2922, 2923, 2916, 2919, 2915, 2920
12/13 June	HM Queen Elizabeth the Queen Mother HRH The Duke of Edinburgh	London Euston–Northallerton (545 miles) Nos 47798 *Prince William* 37079 *Medite*	EWS	2921, 2903, 2904, 2918, 2919, 2914, 2917, 2915, 2920
24/25 June	HRH The Prince of Wales	Gloucester–Preston (440 miles) No 47799 *Prince Henry*	EWS	2921, 2922, 2923, 2919, 2915, 2920
13/14 July	HRH The Prince of Wales	Kemble–Edinburgh (947 miles) No 47798 *Prince William*	EWS	2921, 2922, 2923, 2919, 2915, 2920
18/19 July	HM Queen Elizabeth II HRH The Duke of Edinburgh	London Euston–Derby (426 miles) No 47799 *Prince Henry*	EWS	2906, 2903, 2904, 2918, 2914, 2917, 2915, 2920
24/25 July	HRH The Duke of Edinburgh	London Euston–Plymouth (521 miles) Nos 47798 *Prince William* 47799 *Prince Henry*	EWS	2921, 2904, 2918, 2917, 2915, 2920
6 September	HRH The Prince of Wales HRH Prince William – HRH Prince Henry The Earl Spencer	London Euston–Long Buckby (197 miles) Nos 47798 *Prince William* 47799 *Prince Henry*	EWS	2921, 2918, 2919, 2917, 2920

(Interment of Diana, The Princess of Wales, at Althorp)

1997 *continued*	MEMBER OF THE ROYAL FAMILY/ HEAD OF STATE	JOURNEY DETAILS	RAILWAY OPERATOR	STOCK
21/22 October	HRH The Prince of Wales	Perth–London Euston (904 miles) No 47799 *Prince Henry*	EWS	2921, 2922, 2923, 2919, 2915, 2920
24/27 October	Commonwealth Heads of Government Conference	Edinburgh–Leuchars Leuchars–Edinburgh (966 miles) Nos 47798 *Prince William* 47799 *Prince Henry*	EWS	2906 and VSOE

Date	Member of the Royal Family	Journey details	Railway operator	Stock
27/28 January	HRH The Prince of Wales	Aberdeen–Abergavenny (1,354 miles) Nos 47798 *Prince William* 66187	EWS	2921, 2922, 2923, 2916, 2917, 2915, 2920
16/17 April	HRH The Prince of Wales	Aberdeen–London Euston (1,080 miles) No 47798 *Prince William*	EWS	2921, 2922, 2923, 2916, 2917, 2915, 2920
30 April–2 May	HM Queen Elizabeth II HRH The Duke of Edinburgh	London Euston–Falmouth Docks St Austell–Exeter St Davids Exeter St Davids–Taunton (909 miles) Nos 47798 *Prince William* 47787 *Windsor Castle*	EWS	2921, 2903, 2904, 2918, 2923, 2917, 2915, 2920
6–8 May	HM Queen Elizabeth II HRH The Duke of Edinburgh	Slough–Sunderland Newcastle–Seaham (838 miles) Nos 47798 *Prince William* 47799 *Prince Henry*	EWS	2921, 2903, 2904, 2918, 2923, 2917, 2915, 2920
26–29 May	HM Queen Elizabeth II HRH The Duke of Edinburgh	Wick–Aberdeen Dundee–Edinburgh (1,445 miles) Nos 47798 *Prince William* 47799 *Prince Henry*	EWS	2921, 2903, 2904, 2918, 2923, 2917, 2915, 2920
10–13 June	HM Queen Elizabeth II HRH The Duke of Edinburgh	London Euston–Llanfair PG Llandudno Junction–Dolau Llanelli–Port Talbot Parkway Bridgend–Newport Cardiff Central–London Euston (1,104 miles) Nos 47787 *Windsor Castle* 47798 *Prince William* 4-6-2 No 6233 *Duchess of Sutherland*	EWS	2921, 2903, 2904, 2918, 2923, 2917, 2915, 2920 (99041*)
1–3 July	HM Queen Elizabeth II HRH The Duke of Edinburgh	London Euston–Solihull Birmingham Snow Hill–Birmingham New Street Birmingham New Street–Burton-on-Trent (540 miles) Nos 47798 *Prince William* 47799 *Prince Henry*	EWS	2921, 2903, 2904, 2918, 2923, 2917, 2915, 2920
10–12 July	HM Queen Elizabeth II HRH The Duke of Edinburgh	London Euston–Wakefield Westgate Leeds–Woodlesford Woodlesford–Beverley (642 miles) Nos 47798 *Prince William* 47799 *Prince Henry*	EWS	2921, 2903, 2904, 2918, 2923, 2917, 2915, 2920

2002 *continued*	MEMBER OF THE ROYAL FAMILY	JOURNEY DETAILS	RAILWAY OPERATOR	STOCK
30 July–1 August	HM Queen Elizabeth II	HRH The Duke of Edinburgh London Euston–Scunthorpe Scunthorpe–Nottingham Nottingham–Leicester (578 miles) Nos 47798 *Prince William* 47799 *Prince Henry*	EWS	2921, 2903, 2904, 2918, 2923, 2917, 2915, 2920
4–6 August	HM Queen Elizabeth II HRH The Duke of Edinburgh	Manchester Victoria–Preston Preston–Carlisle Carlisle–Edinburgh Edinburgh–Aberdeen (1,077 miles) Nos 47798 *Prince William* 47799 *Prince Henry*	EWS	2921, 2903, 2904, 2918, 2923, 2917, 2915, 2920
26/27 September	HRH The Prince of Wales	Lairg–Cambridge Nos 47798 *Prince William* 47799 *Prince Henry*	EWS	2921, 2922, 2923, 2916, 2917, 2915, 2920
29/30 September	HRH The Prince of Wales	Kemble–Bradford Forster Square (611 miles) Nos 47798 *Prince William* 47799 *Prince Henry*	EWS	2921, 2922, 2923, 2916, 2917, 2915, 2920
2/3 October	HRH The Prince of Wales	Perth–Maiden Newton (1,122 miles) No 47798 *Prince William*	EWS	2921, 2922, 2923, 2916, 2917, 2915, 2920
23/24 October	HRH The Prince of Wales	Perth–Kirkby Stephen (1,012 miles) No 47798 *Prince William*	EWS	2921, 2922, 2923, 2916, 2917, 2915, 2920
31 October– 1 November	HRH The Duke of Edinburgh	London Euston–Minehead (493 miles) No 47798 *Prince William*	EWS West Somerset Railway	2921, 2904, 2923, 2917, 2915, 2920
8–10 November	HRH The Duke of Edinburgh	London King's Cross–Malton Malton–Spean Bridge (1,136 miles) Nos 47798 *Prince William* 47799 *Prince Henry*	EWS	2921, 2904, 2923, 2917, 2915, 2920
13/14 November	HRH The Prince of Wales	London Euston–Manchester Victoria (410 miles) No 47798 *Prince William*	EWS	2921, 2922, 2923, 2916, 2917 2915, 2920
18/19 November	HRH The Duke of Edinburgh	London Euston–Cardiff Central (391 miles) Nos 47798 *Prince William* 47799 *Prince Henry*	EWS	2921, 2904, 2923, 2917, 2915, 2920

Select Bibliography

Among the books consulted were:

At Home With The Queen, Brian Hoey, Harper Collins, 2002

Dinner in the Diner, Neil Wooler, David & Charles, 1987

Great Western Railway Magazine, 1936

150 Years of Railway Carriages, Geoffrey Kichenside, David & Charles, 1981

Royal Trains, Patrick Kingston, David & Charles, 1985

Royal Trains of the British Isles, *Railway Magazine*, 1974

Royal Travel, Richard Garrett, Blandford Press, 1982

The InterCity Story, edited by Mike Vincent & Chris Green, Oxford Publishing Company, 1994

The Last Journey of King George V, Charles Lee, *Railway Magazine*, 1936

The Moving Force, Bill West, Barracuda Books, 1988

The Railwaymen, Bill West, Barracuda Books, 1986

The Royal Deeside Line, A. D. Farr, David & Charles, 1968

The Royal Trains, C. Hamilton Ellis, Routledge & Kegan Paul, 1975

The Trainmakers, Bill West, Barracuda Books, 1982

Victoria R.I., Elizabeth Longford, Weidenfeld & Nicholson, 1964

Index

Aberdeen Railway 111
Adelaide, Dowager Queen 14, 153
Albert, Prince Consort 19, 106-110, 112, 115, 130, 140
Alexandra, Queen 115-116, 134
Andrew, Prince, Duke of York 143-144
Anne, the Princess Royal 10, 12, 16, 51, 68, 77, 84, 150

Balmoral 19, 34, 51, 110, 112-113, 116
Beatrice, Princess 112, 114
Best, John 143
Bigsby, Bob 23, 44, 48, 50-51, 53
Blair, Cherie 13, 100
Bodmin & Wenford Railway 90
Borain, Josie 124
Branson, Sir Richard 154
British Catering Association 49
British Rail Engineering 142
British Rail Maintenance 142
British Railways/British Rail (BR) 16, 38-39, 78, 85, 121, 142, 147
    Eastern Region 66
    InterCity 88, 150
    InterCity Special Trains 103
    Southern Region 83
    Western Region 66, 143
British Transport Police (BTP) 23, 56, 100, 124
Brunel, Isambard Kingdom 69, 82, 107
Buckingham, Duke of 140
Buckingham Palace 18, 21-22, 50, 52, 60, 66-67, 71, 82, 99-101, 104, 112, 133, 155
Burrell, Paul 124

Carriages 12, 19, 22, 28, 42, 46, 51-52, 57, 60, 67-71, 76-99, 79, 87, 111
    GWR 80, 106, 130, 143
    LMSR 82, 139, 142, 76
    LNER 80
    LNWR 108-110, 112-113, 130, 142
    Pullman cars 79, 83
Carter, Martin 23, 31, 43, 45-46, 48
Charles, Prince of Sweden 133
Charles, Prince of Wales, 10 et seq.
    Duke of Cornwall 17, 70
    Investiture 84-85
Chirac, Bernadette 13
Chretien, Aline 13
Churchill, Sir Winston 79, 82
Clarence House 66, 71, 101
Clinton, Hillary 13
Constantine, Grand Duke of Russia 74
Cornwall, Duchess of 11-12, 15, 17-18, 55, 69-70, 91, 99, 103, 153

Daley, Guy 47
d'Costa, The Duke 132
De Gaulle, General Charles 79
Department of Transport, Local Government and the Regions 11
Diana, Princess of Wales (Lady Diana Spencer) 12, 52, 69, 71, 124-125, 140
Drivers
    Bell, Steve 153
    Court, David 152
    Frosdick, Mick 125
    George, Phil 29, 31-32
    Groves 114
    Hastle, John 108
    Hurst, Jim 107
    Leonard, John 75
Duff, Sir Michael 84

Edward VII, King 14, 19, 74, 108, 115-116, 128, 130-134, 142, 153
    Prince of Wales 115, 130
Edward VIII, King 15, 75, 77
Edwards, Nick 22-24, 29, 31, 49
Elizabeth, The Queen Mother 77, 80, 82, 85-87, 89, 99, 116, 142-143
Elizabeth II HM Queen 10 et seq.
    Coronation 1953 83, 143
    Corgi dogs 34-35
    Diamond Wedding Anniversary 52, 64-65
    Golden Jubilee 2002 11, 35-36, 47-48, 50, 60, 89, 92, 151
    Silver Jubilee 1977 11, 16, 18, 44, 67, 143
English Welsh & Scottish Railway (EWS) 22-23, 27, 32, 36, 40, 56, 59, 64, 89, 92, 99-100, 142, 151
    Toton depot 64, 151
Ernst, Prince of Saxe-Coburg-Gotha 106
Eurostar 53, 154
Exbury Gardens Railway 91

Fellowes, Alexander, Eleanor and Laura 124
Fellowes, Lady Jane 124
Fellowes, Sir Robert 124
First Great Western 16
Forsyth, Thomas 140
Frederick IV, King of Prussia 106-107
Fushima, Prince of Japan 133

Garlick, Geoffrey 143
George V, King 15, 74-75, 101, 116, 134-135
George VI, King 15, 75, 77-78, 116, 118, 126, 140, 142
Gloucester, Duke of 69

Gooch, Daniel 107
Great North of Scotland Railway 116
Great Northern Railway 116
Great Western Railway (GWR) 69, 75, 77, 80, 85, 107-109, 113-114, 116, 130-132, 134-135, 142
    Swindon Works 74-75, 85, 141
Griffiths, Geoff 22, 40, 42, 56-60, 63, 65, 92-93, 99
Griffiths, Pam 42

Haig, Field-Marshal Sir Douglas 75
Harry, Prince 12, 124
Hashimoto, Kumiko 13
Henry, Prince of The Netherlands 132
Hesse, The Grand Duke of 132
Hewlett, Group Captain Timothy 59-60, 151
Highgrove 60, 98
Hillyard, Chris 23, 28-29, 32, 34-35, 55-56, 62-63, 89, 103, 124-125, 146
Holland, Alan 'Dutch' 48
Holt, David 23
Houghton, Gareth 151

Janvrin, Sir Robin 51, 71
Jones, Gareth 49

Kelly, Angela 29, 68
Kent, Duchess of (Worsley, Katherine) 85
Kent, Duke of 78, 85

Leopold, King of The Belgians 107, 132
Leopold, Prince of Saxe-Coburg 132
Locomotives 72
    BR 'Britannia' 70004 *William Shakespeare* 83; 70009 *Alfred the Great* 80; 70030 *William Wordsworth* 83
    BR Class 25 25054 85; 25055 85
    BR Class 47 103; 47528 *The Queen's Own Mercian Yeomanry* 88; 47541 *The Queen Mother* 85, 87; 47620 *Windsor Castle* 85, 92; 47739 *Resourceful* 35; 47787 *Windsor Castle* 92; 47798 *Prince William* 12-13, 89, 91-92, 124, 142; 47799 *Prince Henry* 12-13, 89, 124, 142
    BR Class 91 91029 *Queen Elizabeth II* 88
    BR Class 325 emu 124
    BR(S) Bulleid Pacific 34016 *Bodmin* 79
    BR(W) 'Manor' class 7820 *Dinmore Manor* 91
    EWS Class 66 66187 62
    EWS Class 67 23, 66, 89, 142, 151; 67005

Queen's Messenger 10, 15, 21, 64, 66, 96, 144;
67006 Royal Sovereign 21, 32, 64, 93, 99, 151;
67029 Royal Diamond 18, 32, 64-65, 97-98
    Exmoor Steam Railway 326 Mariloo 91
    GWR 'Atbara' class 3373 Royal Sovereign
128, 156
    GWR Buffalo 108
    GWR 'Castle' class 83; 4082 Windsor
Castle 74-75, 118, 126, 135; 5069 Isambard
Kingdom Brunel 82; 7013 Bristol Castle; 7037
Swindon 85
    GWR Empress of India 114
    GWR 'King' class 6024 King Edward I 50,
102; 6028 King George VI 150
    GWR Phlegethon 107
    GWR 'Star' class 4021 King Edward 132,
134; 4057 Princess Elizabeth 85
    GWR 0-6-0PT 9682 90
    Industrial 0-6-0ST Ugly 90
    LMSR 'Black 5' 44942 82; 44962 82
    LMSR 'Duchess' 6233 Duchess of
Sutherland 36, 55, 59, 92
    LNER A3 class 4472 Flying Scotsman 86
    LNER A4 class 60003 Andrew K. McCosh 82
    LNER B2 class 61671 Royal Sovereign 104
    LNER B17 'Sandringham' class 2800
Sandringham 134; 2847 Helmingham Hall 134
    LNER D16 class 62614 116
    LNWR 2053 Greater Britain 108
    LNWR 'Wolverton Express' Goods' 140
    LNWR 'Wolverton Goods' 0-6-0 141
    LNWR 'Wolverton Tank' 0-4-2 141
    SR 'Schools' class 30915 Brighton 83;
30922 Marlborough 83
London & Birmingham Railway 110, 136,
139-140
London & North Eastern Railway (LNER) 78,
80, 86, 142
London & North Western Railway (LNWR) 14,
41, 52, 75, 106, 108, 113, 134, 139-141
London & South Western Railway (LSWR) 114,
129-131
London, Brighton & South Coast Railway
(LBSCR) 130-131
London, Midland & Scottish Railway (LMS) 24,
76, 78, 82, 103, 142

Mackenzie King, W. L. 79
Maclean, Roderick 74
Malan, Rev. Victor 124
Margaret, Princess 75, 77, 82, 84, 116, 150
Mary, Queen 15, 74-75, 116, 135
Maximilian, Prince of Baden 132
McCorquodale, Emily and George 124
McCorquodale, Lady Sarah 124

Mecklenberg-Strelitz, The Grand Duke
of 133
Midland Railway 110
Millard, Wayne 49
Mitterand, President 53
Moule, Ken 23, 28-29, 34, 40, 43-44, 46,
48, 50-53
Mountbatten, Lord of Burma 18, 120-121

National Railway Museum 89
Network Rail 23-24, 27-28, 56, 63, 99, 152
North Midland Railway 14
North Woolwich Station Museum 86

Osborne House 110, 112, 114, 129-130

Paignton & Dartmouth Railway 102
P&O liner Oriana 35, 52
Parker, Sir Peter 147
Pattenden, Norman 124, 129
Peel, Sir Robert 140
Penny, Roy 68
Persia, Shah of 114
Peters, Peter 75
Philip, Prince (Duke of Edinburgh) 10 et seq.
Pichon, M. 132
Pole, Sir Felix 75
Portugal, King of 107, 132
Prodi, Flavia 13

Queen's Flight, The 17, 151

Radcliffe family 141
RAF No 32 (The Royal) Squadron 17, 59,
97, 151
RailCare 23, 59, 99, 142, 147
Rail Gourmet 19, 36, 38-41, 46-47, 49, 51,
53, 56, 99
Rasputin 115
Richards, Gordon 83
Ross, Jim 49
Roumania, The Crown Prince of 132
Royal Yachts
    Alberta 130
    Britannia 10, 17, 69, 110, 151
    Victoria and Albert 109
Rupert, Prince of Bavaria 132
Russia, Tsar of 112

Sandringham 24, 66, 80, 110, 115-116, 126
Servia, The Crown Prince of 132
Severn Valley Railway 102-103

Shand-Kydd, The Hon. Mrs 124
Smuts, General Jan 79
Snowdon, Earl of 85
South Eastern Railway 74
South Eastern & Chatham Railway 75
South West Trains 53
Southern Railway (SR) 78-79, 142
Spencer, Earl 12, 124, 140
Stephenson, Robert 136, 147

Talyllyn Railway 91
Tebbutt, Colin 124

Venice Simplon-Orient-Express 103, 150
Victoria, Princess 114
Victoria, Queen 14, 19, 63, 74-75, 104, 106,
108-115, 128-134, 140, 143-144, 154
    Diamond Jubilee 1897
    Empress of India 114
Virgin Trains 38, 40, 44, 48, 101

Wellington, Duke of 140
Welsh Assembly 55
Wessex, Earl of 12
West Coast Railway Co. 89
West Somerset Railway 91, 102
Westminster Abbey 83, 124, 126
Wilhelm II, Kaiser, His Imperial Majesty
the German Emperor, 128, 131, 134
William, Prince 12, 124, 155
William IV, King 14
Williams, Roger 36, 38-40, 44, 47-48, 52-53
Windsor 14, 22, 50-51, 82, 101, 104, 106,
109, 129-130, 133
Winkworth, Mark 125
Wolverton depot and works 22-24, 49-50,
56, 59, 67, 71, 76, 78, 89, 103, 113, 124-125,
136-147

Yeltsin, Naina 13
York, Duke of 12